WHO KILLED KASHEER?

WHO KILLED KASHEER?

RUHAIL KHAN

Notion Press

Old No. 38, New No. 6
McNichols Road, Chetpet
Chennai - 600 031

First Published by Notion Press 2017

ISBN
Hardcase: 978-1-947283-08-4
Paperback: 978-1-947283-09-1

ABOUT THE AUTHOR

Ruhail is a Top Management professional and an industry thought leader. He considers himself as "work in progress." He is spell-bound by the magnificence of creation and is deeply committed to human conflict resolution, upholding the sanctity of life and tolerant co-existence of all strains of humanity in an ethos of mutual respect and dignity.

Besides being a voracious reader and a prolific writer, he juggles his spare time to indulge in his passions of long-distance swimming, trekking, travelling, conservation and fulfilling his diverse socio-cultural obligations. His other personal interests include comparative theology, fiqh, music, cooking, technology, philosophy, psychology, world history, anthropology, warfare and defense systems, international relations and global polity; though not necessarily in this order.

But what he loves doing the most is to spend time and have fun with his family. He currently lives with his wife and two daughters in Mumbai.

CONTENTS

Preface .... *xi*

Acknowledgments .... *xiii*

I remember 01

Where has the glory gone? 14

Who killed Kasheer? 18

Twins of fate 32

Kashmiriyat 37

Crackdown! 39

Oh! Daughters of Eve 42

Precocious buds 52

Sad flows the Jhelum 54

Two sides of a coin 57

Soanth 61

Kashur 64

What if 68

Baptism 73

Kasher Koor 76

The conch that fell silent 78

Sangbaaz 83

Time 86

Hope and beyond 87

Youp 91

Wande 94

Half's and None's 97

An Ode to the alphabets of Kashur stoicism 103

Glossary *127*

PREFACE

I've never been immune to the trials, travails, and tribulations of Kashmir. I've personally witnessed the loss, pain, and suffering of the masses; the epochal cultural transformation and the institutionalization of barbarity aided by draconian laws. I've been privy to episodes of degradation, denigration, and denial of human rights and the attendant nonchalant dismissal of the dignity of human life.

Over the years, I've seen young lives snatched, honor ravaged, dreams scuttled, futures obscured, livelihoods threatened, justice denied, accountability ignored, experiences tainted, psyches traumatized, communities uprooted, and media-driven stereotypes, especially the bogey of Islamism and Islamic Jihad; reinforced and entrenched across the gullible and information-starved masses countrywide.

The world's most militarized tinderbox, with an active deployment of approximately 1,000,000 armed forces; and mismanaged by a concatenation of self-perpetuating, corrupt, and inefficient local polity and a mélange of local and central bureaucracy, has been held hostage by history, imperialism, geo-strategic posturing, religio-political affiliations, economic compulsions, and popular sentiment.

A smorgasbord of resistance and militant entities has compounded the working dynamic of the imbroglio. The decades gone by have been spectators to the various transformations of this narrative which have impacted the nature and course of these entities and the cavalcade of events triggered till date. The latest accoutrement to the canvass has been an almost unending spate of street protests.

The preponderance of global conflicts has largely obscured this ongoing turmoil which has so far claimed more than 100,000 dead and thousands more missing, maimed, blinded, tortured, and incarcerated while some being "discovered" in mass graves with a disturbing consistency. In this jeremiad of loss, it's immaterial to pinpoint either accountability or complicity of the various stakeholders involved.

I took it upon myself as a moral and social obligation to showcase the real Kashmir; beautiful, battered, brutal; as opposed to political PR ops, TRP-driven media machinations and stereotypical Bollywood fantasies loaded with falsehoods, misrepresentations, and episodes of alternate truth. Every Kashmiri is a protagonist, every event a representation and every experience an illustration in this "all-inclusive" and "true-to-life" poetic exposition.

The journey of writing this volume has been one of painful catharsis and self-realization. I hope that you shall find it as encompassing, engrossing, and enlightening as I have…

ACKNOWLEDGMENTS

I've always believed that creative expositions are precipitated by inspirational episodes. However, I chose to ignore the calling for quite some time to my own peril till my wife, *Sheema, [Sheemu for me]* got the better of me. She's been overwhelming in her inspiration and relentless in her encouragement and hence this book. I love and cherish her for what she is; *as the love of my life, my anchor and of course, my most scathing critic too.* And yes, it would have been unimaginable for me to write this book without the love and affection of my two beautiful daughters, *Zinneerah and Zunnairah,* who adapted to the constraints of my time and unwitting deficits in attention remarkably well. *I love you ZinZun.*

It would be insane to miss this opportunity to thank my parents, *Late Mr. A.M. Khan [Aba] and Mrs. Gulshan Khan [Mummy],* for grooming me the way that I have turned out to be and my grandparents for being there whenever I felt constrained in my understanding of this world.

And well, yes, I want to relish this moment as I convey my love and gratitude to my in-laws, *Dr. G.M. Jan [Abu] and Dr. Haseena Akhtar [Mamma]* who've loved me enough to rekindle and reinforce my belief in human relationships and their sanctity.

It goes without saying that I'm absolutely awed by my superbly creative and dedicated publishing team that was there with me at every stage of this book and helped me transform my endeavours into reality.

I REMEMBER

I remember…

The first rays of sun unshackling themselves,
from the unrelenting vice of gloomy darkness…
Gleefully unfolding like an incessant struggle,
of behemoths caught in perennial battle…
Victorious, they'd appear as radiant angels,
fluttering their mighty wings of glorious light…
Indomitable, like dazzling knights ,
galloping on their illuminated and unbridled steeds…
The mountain tops of Zabarwan would glisten,
with an imposing canopy of pristine white…
And the foliage bursting in myriad kaleidoscopes,
of colour and form as a spectacular sight…
The ethereal dew on the luscious petals of fragrant blossoms,
cloaking their chaste beauty…
A never ending virginal drape,
consciously hiding the mysteries of their mesmerizing charm…

The call of the muezzins from Hazratbal,
would reverberate as ripples across the lake…
Like a divine rhapsody playing mellifluously,
in the deepest recesses of dreams…
Soon the bells at Shankaracharya would resonate,
across the sprawling Takht-e-Sulaiman…
Like little flat stones swirling and skimming,
as racing comets across the morning sky…

Forlorn cocks crowing their hearts out,
in valiant attempts to shake all out of their slumber…
And the crickets stuttering into silence,
like kids cuddled by fairies to enchanted sleep…
Birds of all genre perched on every trunk,
and inside every dark nook and safe cranny…
Ceaselessly chirping in a symphony of obeisance,
to the glory of the Magnificent Creator…

The radiant waves of light proudly engulfing,
the gardens crafted by the Mughals in love…
As the magical retreats of the proud mortals,
would succumb in awe to glorious Nature…
Masterpieces all, from the decrepit Pari Mahal,
and the lofty gardens of Chashma Shahi…
To the heavenly Nishat and Shalimar,
all glowing in a coruscating efflorescence of beauty…
Soon they'll be merrily tip-toeing like effulgent fairies,
on the placid waters of the Dal…
Transforming this lotus-pond into a bedazzling portrait,
of an enchantress hued in gold…
Time standing still and relishing,
this fervently sought out hiatus from due evanescence…
Making an Emperor sigh,
"If there is a paradise on earth, it is here, it is here, it is here"…

The fluttering of humungous flocks of pigeons,
at Kabootar Khana; a relic of the days gone by…
A gaggle of geese, a badling of ducks,
a murder of crows, and a ballet of swans overhead…
A grist of bees, a host of sparrows,
a party of jays, and a tittering of magpies up ahead …

A repetitive scene played straight out of a composition,
aiming for its altaltissimo in finality...
The vegetables harvested from the Radh,
and the flowers loaded on Shikaras by womenfolk...
Like water-nymphs carrying sacred offerings,
to sustain life in the hallowed realms of yore...
The abiding chinars at Char-Chinari getting emblazoned,
once again in three centuries of being...
Sombre and dignified in contemplation,
like the Pharoahs chiselled in stone at Abu Simbel...

The houseboats on the Dal would appear,
like venerable sculptures in cedar and honey...
As proud monuments of luxurious craftsmanship,
claiming their rightful place in history...
The soothing rustle of the shikarawallahs' oars,
would testify to their indefatigable spirit...
Crafting passages of opportunity and optimism,
in the generous waters by divine will...
The wafts of invigorating breeze would coerce,
an optimistic niche in the unsure soul...
And the tingling warmth of the blessed mornings suffuse,
the struggling mind with hope...
The smoke rising from the Doonga chimneys,
and quaint little hutments on the hills...
Would quietly herald the birth of one more seduction by life,
and augur insatiable desire...

04 / WHO KILLED KASHEER? / Ruhail Khan

I remember…

The beckoning of the dew-decked carpet of cold morning grass,
for the first trepiditious steps…
That would naughtily entice and embolden,
the amorous tingling of pliant soles and the spine……
Gold-plates, Monkshoods, Lady's mantles, and Marguerites,
Columbines, Thrifts, Brocades, and Asters…
Goldilocks, Begonias, Bergenias, and Kingcups,
Lavenders, Bellflowers, Cinquefoils, and Chrysanthemums…
Delphiniums, Carnations, Gingers, and Geraniums,
Gerberas, Roses, Sunflowers, and Hellebores…
Hibiscus, Inulas, Lupins, and Phloxes,
Violets, Primroses, Daisies, and Paeonias…
The misty air would be heavily redolent,
with an enrapturing bouquet of bewitching fragrances…
Enchanting the senses to whirl into a frenzied trance,
like a swirling Turkish dervish in ecstasy…

Feeding the precocious school of fish in the pellucid pond,
as they braved the wiles of swirling water…
And savouring the gushing and gurgling of the feisty stream,
tingling like a carol of silver bells…
Spread out like a Vitruvian man on the plush velvet,
to banish the demons of human undoing…
A cavalcade of strange shapes trailing across,
with eyes squinting to avoid the blinding glare of sun…
The birds would cackle and fly away in magical murmurations,
as if under a charlatans spell…
And the mind would create images of angels and demons,
in the innocuous clouds passing by…

It would appear as if somehow Bach and Beethoven,
have together taken Centrestage to enthrall…
Flabbergasting the audience with a fusion,
of the six Brandenburg concertos and Nine symphonies…

The euphoria would be interrupted by the mouthwatering aromas,
arrogantly diffusing through the veil…
Weaving and wading their way across the enriched air,
to tease the already saturated senses…
A shrill call from within would beckon you,
to make nimble footsteps your reliable companion…
Excitement and anticipation easing your surrender,
to relish the creations of the chef-de-cuisine…
The traditional spread would appear like a fantasy,
concocted from a gourmet's magical recipes…
And the experience evoking an edifying rapture,
for a capricious connoisseur and a commoner too…
The culinary repertoire, the precedents of fabled hospitality,
and the prerogative of presence…
All of them colluding to create indelible episodes,
and enduring memories for a lifetime to come…

The onset of summer and the countless blossoms,
the long sunny days and the short starry nights to woo…
The weekend movies on TV and the latest cassettes,
of Boney M, ABBA, AC/DC, and George Michael in tow…
Reading the latest Indrajal and ACK comics,
hidden in practical notebooks, and rare Commando comics too…
The plans for summer vacation and shopping lists,
scribbled and slashed across with some personal secrets too…
The passing of spring and summer,
like a dream one desperately wanted to get back into but couldn't…

Leaving behind a lingering feeling of incompleteness,
a void, an emptiness that carries itself onwards…
The onset of autumn, the chinars on fire,
the withering of trees, and the carpets of faded leaves everywhere…
The listless sun, the morose skies, the fallow fields,
and the clouds of smoke billowing across fields and atop hills…

The dropping temperatures, the chill permeating the air,
the short days, and the never-ending nights…
The first snowfall, the icicles lurking dangerously overhead,
the frozen taps, and the first sheen-e-jung…
The stockpiling of dried vegetables and fish,
tonnes of clothing, freezing beds, with crushing quilts…
The shy sun and recalcitrant vehicles,
these heralds of winter would be dreaded first and enjoyed later…
The kahwa and noon-chai with sheermal in the morning,
with heavy lunches and, light dinners at night…
The munching on nadr-e-monji and monje gaade,
the wicked scoops of sheen-e-kulfi, and ice cream…
The huddling together at night under the light of ubiquitous gas lights,
to be regaled by legends of yore…
About princes, princesses, and evil divs in Shahnameh,
or the heartbreaking tales from Kashur folklore...

I remember…

The incessant chaos and the interminable cacophony outside,
that would do the tower of Babel proud…
The multitudinous markets appearing as medieval middle-eastern souks,
transported magically back in time…
The queue at the ubiquitous Kanderwaan,
would be a perfect example of equality and humility…
As the crowds engaged in banter and chatter around the tandoor,
would cut across caste and class…
Similar sights at the Goorewaan, Pujwaan and Danderwaan,
would reinforce the real social network…
The condolences, good wishes on a kid's birth,
the get well soon messages, and queries of concern…
The announcement of engagements, updates on scandals,
and the debates on politics getting hotter…
All this and more creating episodes of camaraderie,
forged in mutual respect, love, and acceptance…

A pack of fattened canines eyeing a frightened kid's bread,
and the bold crows diving in for the kill…
Remnants of a pack of squashed mice on the road,
as evidence of the blood thirst of a clowder of cats…
The wary pigeons plucking one grain at a time,
and a flight of shy swallows perched on power lines…
A majestic eagle swooping in disdain from nowhere,
to claim the lifeless rodents as its inalienable right…
The disgruntled sweepers earnestly trying make sense,
of what usually appear as roads and alleyways…
Clogged drains, mounds of trash and over spilled bins,
making navigation through the mess an exalted art…

Kids and teens, fearful of the Maulvi's rod,
taking brisk steps to the nearest madrassa or mosque on time...
To acquaint their minds and purify their souls,
with Ilm-i-Din and the repetitive hum of Quranic recitations...

The clanging of metal as the shop-shutters would be rolled up,
to begin a fresh tryst with sustenance...
The enthusiastic dusting of wares, sweeping of the floors,
and washing of the pavements as a daily ritual...
The harried hawkers setting up and often wrapping up,
their displays at the whims of corrupt policemen...
And some privileged ones retaining their spots for years on end,
as you stumble across them after ages...
The Rediwallahs vying with each other to net the office goers,
students, daily-wagers, and shopkeepers too...
With their ever-boiling pots of tea, pyramids of boiled eggs,
and neatly laid out Puffs and Bakirkhwanis...
Proud beggars, desperate beggars, habitual beggars,
urbane beggars, visiting beggars, and relentless beggars...
Destitute women hiding in tattered burkhas,
and snotty kids pushed in the trade who test your conscience...

From the cluttered shops in Shehr-e-Khaas,
to the high-end showrooms lined up at Poloview and Residency...
Exotic carpets, priceless Shahtoosh, snobbish Pashminas,
sober Dussas, ethereal silks and cozy Namdas too ...
Intricately hand-carved masterpieces, regal walnut wood furniture,
cascading crewel upholstery, and curtains...

And delicate Papier-Mâché pieces, elegant embroidery,
exquisite copper utensils, and sought out knick-knacks…
All of them proud exhibits of legendary Kashmiri craftsmanship,
and testaments to the ingenuity of the Kashur…
What with a canvass long dubbed as the world's most beautiful,
offering gratuitous inspiration in abundance…
Greenhorns to veterans, the shopkeepers would unleash their irresistible charm,
on natives and foreigners alike…
Haggling for a hundred to offering their products for free,
disarming their resistance over a cup of Kahwa or tea…

Vehicles of all descriptions manoeuvring their way,
through a swarm of ordered chaos on streets and bylanes…
Apologetic honks, ear-splitting honks, sadistic honks,
belching honks, stuttering honks and squeaking honks …
All trying in vain to cajole, convince or coerce,
the nawabs of the roads to ignore their egos and make some way…
Snorting horse's clonking to pull the rare Tongas,
and a kine of bellowing bovines lazily surveying the realm…
Herds of sheep and goats whipped to bleat, butt, and badger,
in a frightened scurry and a brood of hens nearby…
Matadors and Mazda's chasing each other and halting,
wherever they feel to pick up passengers and drop none…
And in this mad melee, like a breath of fresh air,
would appear little cherubs from heaven escorted by parents…
Kids, comme il faut, feigning confidence or forcibly weaned,
as they outdo each other to climb up and grab a seat...

I remember…

The best days of my childhood, the fun–filled school days,
right from kindergarten to the secondary school…
From being pulled out of bed to catching a quick breakfast,
donning school uniforms to acting snobbish…
The early morning rush to catch the school bus,
and the secret glee on feigning an illness once in a while…
A tour of the city and the sights to behold,
time to read a Phantom comic or flip through a Hardy Boys novel…
The singing of the hymns, felicitations on stage,
the grooming checks, and updating of news board without fail…
The pranks in the labs, the attentiveness in the lectures,
the burdensome homework to be completed at home…
Erudite teachers, skilled teachers, venerable teachers,
autocratic teachers, boring teachers, and some funny ones too…
All potters of yore, moulding our personalities, and sharpening our intellect,
like malleable lumps of pregnant clay…

The scampering to the canteen, the shared warm lunches,
the sewaiyan kulfi on the other side of the picket fence…
The boring medical check-ups, the dreaded vaccinations,
the visits to the Leper Colony, apt lessons in humanity…
The daily visits to the library and the tours of the museum,
the buildings of models and charts to adorn the walls…
The weekly house games and the regattas on Wednesdays,
the tiring swims in the staid Dal crisscrossing its length …
The Zabarwan climbs and Twin peaks too,
a yearly ritual alongwith the weeklong camps to the hypnotic margs…
The treks to Mahadev, hikes to Sunset and Sunrise peaks,
camping at Kaunsarnag, Alapather, and Gangabal too…

The setting up of tents and digging of drainage trenches,
the queues in the camp mess, and fun at campfires due...
The friendships made and brotherhood created,
to forever live the credo honourably, "In all things be men"...

Recitations of poetry, declamations, and debates,
essay writing competitions, skits, and annual drama in tow...
The cross country runs shaking all out of wintry slumber,
and snaking up the Sulaiman like penguins out to sea...
The athletic competitions and preparations for the parent's day,
all worth their salt jumping in the fray for glory...
The unshackled raging hormones,
the conspicuous awareness of appearance with trimmed hair and goatees ...
The desire to excel and be the best,
the competitive streak and winners' habit, egged on by the contenders all...
The fun projects in the summer vacations,
the burning of midnight oil in winters to be one ahead of the pack...
The voracious gorging of books and rummaging through encyclopedias,
memorizing atlases, and memoirs in sync...
The weekly revisions and monthly tests, annual results with heartbreaks,
with awards'n' accolades for deserving few...

The chole bhatoorey at Shakti and SantRam,
the mango shakes at Erina, and the hot chilli-chicken at Shamiyana...
The pastries at Jee Enns, the tea at LalaSheikhs,
the patties and cakes at Mughal durbar, and the coffee at Zero Inn...
The hogging of Seekh Tuji at Khayam or the Boulevard,
the scrumptious Masala Lavasa rolls on the stairs of the Bund...
The Mutton Kanti at Tao and Kebabs at Mehfil,
the Harissa from Ali Kadal, and Ama Baedaene Kulfi at Bohri Kadal...
The refreshing drives on the Boulevard, the idyllic shikara rides,
and the fun of diving from the swimming boats...

The shortcuts to downtown through a maze of serpentine alleys,
serendipitous bylanes, and crumbling houses in rows…
The evening hikes to Dara Shukoh's library,
the mimicry of ghosts and fairies, and tales untold across time…
The nocturnal drives to Pampore, the saffron blooms under the full moon,
the breathtaking landscape carved in silver…

The night long Shab-e-Qadr and Baraat prayers at Hazratbal or Jamia,
climbing up the stairs at Makhdoom Sahib…
The yearly trips to Chrar-i-Sharif and shopping for ornamental Kangris,
the regular attendance at Dastgeer Sahib…
The gaiety of Eids and salivations for Eidi,
the rearing of sheep for qurbani, and the eagerness to distribute the same…
The hospitality of relatives, the slobbered kisses on faces,
the bear hugs, and the cramped stomachs crying "No more"
The festivities at home, a celebration of faith, appetizing barbeques,
and lavish spreads tempting the taste buds…
The crackle of fireworks, Rouf in the background,
the strains of Shameem Dev's "Mati Roze "wafting through the din.
The late night dinners, gathering of friends and family,
reliving of experiences, and generous dole outs of wisdom…
The counting of stars, the wishes made, the secrets shared,
and the dreams conjured under the canopy of the star-lit sky…

And of course,

The family trips to Gulmarg, the stays at Highlands,
the horse rides, and treks to Khilanmarg and back...
The putts at the golf-course and the Gondola rides,
the pinecone collecting, and rolling down on meadows...
The picnics on the banks of Lidder at Pahalgam,
the long walks to Aru, and the hikes to the twins at Tarsar and Marsar...
The caravans of Gujjars, pitching tents on the riverbanks,
the fire in the hearths, and strumming of the Rhubabs...
The Shikara rides in the serene Manasbal Lake,
and the gorging on sumptuous lunches on the banks of Indus at Prang...
The drives along scary, winding roads to Yusmarg,
the finger licking chicken, and paranthas at the TDC huts...
The heavenly trips to Kokernag and Verinag,
the reflecting in the solitude at Daksum, and Aharbal falls...
The trips to Wular lake and humbled at its magnificence,
the stopovers at Sonamarg, a divine experience...

Ah!

The visions of the future, the aspirations entertained, the choices imposed, and the expectations loaded...
The decisions made and the efforts put in, the realizations affected, and the achievements appreciated...
The careers selected, the exodus for sustenance creating a diaspora of Atlases arching under their earths...
The accord with manhood and the transition of responsibilities with crosses to carry, for one and all...
The acclimatization with weather, the endeavours to carve a niche in disparate and prejudiced environs...
The long distance calls back home, the funerals in absentia, and the fleeting attendances at marriages...
The microcosms of culture and the strict paradigms of tradition created and guarded in lands afar...
The perennial longing, the eternal pride, the plausible justifications, and the elusive reminiscences...

Oh, yes...I remember it all...

WHERE HAS THE GLORY GONE?

Civilization is at the crossroads,
of inclusivity and isolation…
History has been archived,
in the annals of ignorance…

Culture stands eroded,
at the altar of revisionism…
Legacy bequeathed has been lost,
in the winds of change…

Humanity has been exiled,
to depths of ignominy…
Human dignity has been effaced,
by the surfeit of tyranny…

Innocence has been lost,
to the onslaught of barbarity…
Ethics have been disposed off,
in the marshes of temptation…

Civility has vanished,
under the pretext of empowerment…
Virtue has become suspect,
due to the preponderance of immorality…

Principles have been buried,
in the corridors of power…
Precepts have become inconsequential,
in the conduct of public life…

Prejudices are rampant,
across every segment of society...
Misconceptions are rife,
as clarity becomes objectified...

Tolerance has been banished,
to the abyss of no-return...
Every freedom is threatened,
at the stake of fascism...

Etiquette has vanished,
in the pursuit of enrichment...
Love has been hijacked,
by lust and lasciviousness...

Brotherhood has been replaced,
by one-upmanship...
Friendships have been overtaken,
by greed and self- interest...

The cause has been hijacked,
by a coterie of self-perpetuators...
Sympathy has fallen short,
of living up to expectations...

Empathy is sorely missing,
in a culture of self-centredness...
Honesty is despised,
as a stumbling block in progress...

Truth has been vandalized,
as a victim of manipulation…
Intellectualism has been chastised,
by retards ruling the roost…

Morality has been compromised,
at the edifice of modernity…
Character has ceased to be strength,
as it is considered dispensable now…

Esprit de corps melted away,
In the heat of self-glorification…
Steadfastness has evaporated,
into the thin air of compromise…

Misconceptions are rife,
as clarity becomes objectified…
Accomplishments have been shorn off,
by the burnishings of mediocrity…

Solidarity has vanished,
behind the veneer of limitations…
Altruism is being castigated,
as a display of weakness…

Meritocracy has been sold,
in the bazaars of nepotism and sycophancy…
Freewill has been tied up,
in the labyrinths of repression…

Courage has been hijacked,
by a mindset of despondency…
Faith has been sacrificed,
at the gates of pretence…

Justice has faltered,
on the track of appeasement…
The state has failed,
to live up to its premise…

Where has the glory gone?

WHO KILLED KASHEER?

Saints flocked to you in droves…
Conquerors fought for you across the ages…
Emperors swooned in ecstasy beholding you…
Poets waxed eloquent about your beauty…

Towering mountains infused humility…
Pristine lakes offered tranquility…
Lush meadows instilled hope…
Verdant forests accorded contemplation…

Majestic rivers sustained life…
Ethereal waterfalls evoked passion…
Limpid pools mesmerized minds…
Gurgling streams echoed divine rhapsodies…

Rich fields staved off hunger…
Bountiful orchards tempted the senses…
Perennial blossoms healed the souls…
Rouf and Wanvun celebrated innocence...

Chiru draped the Aristocracy…
And Changthangi challenged the Vicuna…
Commoners make did with the Poatsch…
Landed flaunted the Karakuli with Dusse…

Legendary Kashyapa got credited with your habitation…
Kalhana recorded your journey in hyperbole…
Kanishka embedded Buddhism …
Mihirakula stamped terror on their hearts…

Umayyad's exposed you to Islam...
Somanand surfaced with Shaivism...
Lalitaditya held sway till Magadha...
Abhinavagupta eulogized kaula and trika...

Rinchana became Sadruddin impressed by Bulbul Shah's way
And Shamsuddin established the first Muslim Sultanate...
Amir-i-Kabir suffused you with Islam...
Along with Yogi Shahpore and ten-thousand more ...

Fakes and claimants, a thousand Sayyids found refuge...
Tamerlane had chilled their spines with impending scourge...
The masses shaken out of their pagan slumber...
Minds prepped up and souls ready to deliver...

Mosques and Khanekahs dotted your breast...
A conscience stirred and never laid to rest...
Azaan and Awrad resonated across the realm...
Prayer and passion did every obstacle overwhelm...

A syncretic creed appeared on the horizon...
Kashmiriyat ensured a welcome for every denizen...
Enlightened souls scuttled exclusion...
Camaraderie prevailed above every denomination...

Lal Ded immortalized herself by her Vakh...
Nund Reshi guided the souls through his Shrukhe...
Habba Khatoon eternalized Lol...
Later Arnimaal followed a similar goal...

Sikandar in his zeal became But-Shikan...
Zain-ul-Abidin did reveal himself as BadShah...
Kalima and conch reverberated side by side...
Superstitions and evil practices were put aside...

Culture flowered like never before…
Granaries brimmed over with farmers' smiles and more…
Trade flourished and so did arts and crafts…
Carpets, Papier Machie, Calligraphy, and Shawls…

Yusuf Shah resisted the might of Mughals…
Victorious twice but treachery prevailed…
Masters changed and Durrani's came to the fore…
On Pandits shoulders the Afghans crossed ashore…

Sikhs scaled up the spectre of tyranny…
Dogras earned a reprehensible infamy…
Azaan was banned and the Jamia locked…
Men, women, and land they pillaged all…

Men sent for begar…
Women to the harem…
Every trade taxed to its death…
Oldest profession and grave digging too…

The landscape bleak the tidings grim…
The grail of patience tipped over the brim…
Repression ruled and injustice thrived…
For evil, the moment of truth had arrived...

Resistance took root in your soil…
You had your martyrs toil…
Cries turned into a crescendo…
Emancipation boasted of a divine halo…

As evil was in throes of death…
Preying vultures primed their beaks…
Neither religion nor ideology could tilt the scales…
But lies and deception hid behind their veils…

Out there India burned but you stood tall...
Muslims or otherwise, you cradled all...
Shone like a beacon in a sea of blood...
Gandhi praised as lives were carried away by wood...

The days of reckoning were indeed near...
Your notion of freedom some couldn't bear...
By hook or crook, they wanted to ensnare...
Your soul and flesh, primed to shred and tear...

Every paradise has its serpent...
How could you be any different...
They came from everywhere...
Big, small, and haywire...

Standstill, Independence, Accession all got inked...
But your Kashur had his aspirations jinxed...
Mountbatten, Pandit, Patel and the Lion...
Linked it to free will of Kashur in that eon...

The wizard cast his dice...
And called some more vice...
They promised not to sting...
But integrity was not their thing...

Arson, mayhem, rape, and blood...
Death and destruction followed everywhere they could...
Frenzied talks for promises to build...
Nobody atoned as there was no guilt...

Change of guard offered some hope...
Raghu Ram Kaul's Sheikh held your reins...
The wizard had fled like Suhadeva before...
The pretender retained as a point to score...

The lion couldn't fathom the deep sea...
Neither could he brave the abyss...
Intrigue, deceit, lies, and half-truths...
Back-stabbing shrouded as Conspiracy Case...

Back to the cage said the Pandit with a frown...
You had a new king wear the crown...
Bakshi did you some good...
Sadiq and Qasim couldn't make anybody proud...

Twice again the deep sea and abyss bled...
A part shorn, a part shred...
Families split and bonds melt...
Massacres happened that nobody felt...

The Aatish in the Chinar had turned to dust...
Will and trust surrendered to rust...
Once more your blood betrayed by illicit lust...
A dagger thrust deep in your magnanimous chest...

Dilli as usual scripted the puppet show...
Boots marched in with a new tyranny in tow...
Plebiscite, Referendum, Autonomy, and Independence a strict NO...
Your "Pir-e-Vaer" lost its divine glow...

The philanderer came and went, now and again...
Intoxicated by power, notoriety did he gain...
Fickle as sand and loyal as an adder...
Clung to nettle to hold the sceptre...

Resentment, frustration, helplessness, and anger...
Options to explore were loaded with danger...
Deceit, exclusion, isolation, and exploitation...
Tehreek, militancy erupted as the manifestation...

"Hum Kya Chahtey" became your new anthem...
"Jago, Jago Subeh huwi" blared from the minarets...
Op Tupac got a new Avatar...
You braced yourself for an unfamiliar war...

Across fields and atop every hill...
In the streets and from every window sill...
Cities, towns, and villages remote...
"Azadi", "Azadi" did everyone promote...

Folks rallied to create you a new Charter...
Men and women accepted the dangerous barter...
Soon they swelled the ranks to be a martyr...
The spirit of loss and sacrifice it did garner...

Off in droves, the youth slipped across...
Braved the mountains and treacherous sloths...
Ignored hunger, pain, suffering, and loss...
Knowing little that they were pawns of a toss...

Love, respect, and admiration showered...
With fear and uncertainty the meek cowered...
Their Legend spread like ocean swell...
Soon the Deep Sea unleashed hell...

In every house and at Hazratbal...
Your Kashur feared his own cannibal...
Faith was lost and the halo gone...
That loss of innocence, you still mourn...

Vendetta, greed, power, and disrespect...
What started as divine turned into a futile quest...
The gullible and innocent, most of them fell...
Spineless turncoats helmed this version of Hell...

"Crack Down" and "Cross Firing", additions to your lexicon...
Few moments of calm in a day were the new halcyon...
AK's, LMG's, RPG's, and IED's *et al*...
The sane disenchanted but kids in thrall...

Funds for Tanzeem, funds for the mosque...
Abuse of the commoner, evil and grotesque...
Lunch for a dozen and dinner with caution...
Decency and civility, a non-existent notion...

Curfew and hartal choked off sustenance...
For succor and solace, you begged providence...
Fear and uncertainty ruled the roost...
A generation lost was what you could boast...

The home breds petered out into inconsequence...
You again witnessed Cain killing Abel in vengeance...
Fervour and fanaticism replaced the old order...
The Kashur once more became cannon fodder...

A head-priest murdered here and a head-priest killed there...
A scholar decapitated here and a doctor there...
Schools burnt and not a bridge to spare...
Roads to progress, laid tattered and bare...

The right-wing apparatchik was the spearhead...
In every nook and corner you identified dread...
Cold, clinical, and barbaric was the reprisal...
Detention, torture, rape, and killing didn't need approval...

TADA, AFSPA, PSA were the spawn of terror...
Many a youth did in their wake wither...
Staying alive became a cherished dream...
You shivered with fear to hear your masses scream...

Some temples burnt, some idols desecrated...
Some killed and many felt endangered...
The apparatchik fuelled fear with his wickedness...
Exodus cost the brethren their innocence...

Seers of learning left without their earnings...
Torn apart from their hearth with yearnings...
Sympathy, empathy, and pretense of brotherhood...
The diaspora, alone and unsheltered, understood the truth...

An ethnicity uprooted, a culture torn apart...
Knowledge and beauty did furtively depart...
Tulmul awaited the devotees and Shankaracharya too...
Hari-Parbat wasn't thronged and Mattan left unattended too...

Neighbours since ages, friends for a lifetime...
Defiant lovers braved censure, their love sublime...
Tutors and pupils, the debt never repaid...
Herath Walnuts and subtle wit, perpetually mourned...

General and Spook in two stints each...
Crafted a strategy to increase their morbid reach...
Outwitted and moribund were the cut throat tribes...
Gutless parasites living off the devil's bribes...

JIC's, PAPA 2 and their ilk along with the encounter...
Dismemberment and death, the only rejoinder...
Mukhbir, CAT, Judas, Fawkes, and Quislings too...
Posthumous kids, half's, none's and senescence stared at you...

Boots in the mosques, boots on the chests...
Boots in the houses, boots on the breasts...
Boots in the blossoms, boots on the harvests,
Boots in the orchards, boots on the crests...

Blood on the streets, blood in the drains…
Blood in the fields, blood on the hillocks…
Blood on the floors, blood in the marshes…
Blood in the rivers, blood on the stairs…

Headless bodies, hollow bodies…
Carved bodies, charred bodies…
Mutilated bodies, unidentified bodies…
Buried bodies, drowned bodies…

They turned you into an abysmal mortuary…
Of lives cut short and futures blurry…
Where optimism and hope were crucified in a hurry…
And maelstroms of loss, scamper and scurry…

A superpower made inconsequential…
A battle hardened nation again proved its credential…
Alas! To the Abyss, a debt to be honored…
For brinksmanship and hatred, sanity ignored…

The barbarian horde, still looking for gold…
Started with a trickle, soon turned manifold…
Village after village and town after town,
Ravished and ravaged, your fabric was torn…

Unkempt, uncouth, and unlettered beasts of prey…
Tried to impose unsanctimonious precepts, long in decay…
Offered you no leeway, leave alone your miseries allay…
Their vanity and blood lust scripted their doomsday…

Chrar-i-Sharif gutted and the sanctuary up in smoke…
That was the day the enchantment broke…
The die was cast for the immoral dagger and cloak…
Aliens, Mlecchas would barbarity no longer stoke…

Dark terror spread its tentacles ...
Renegades, Ikhwan, SOG appeared in an eye blink...
The Lernaean Hydra had death to milk...
Nothing stayed sacred in the land of silk...

Extortion, rape, disappearance, and death...
Paroxysms of justice, a mere shibboleth...
With a prayer and fear in every breath...
Dignity of life, a tattered wreath...

Battered Che's found solace in the Grecian norm...
Firebrands, moderates did a brotherhood form...
From the pulpits and the Mehrab...
Panelled parlours and in every garb...

Some spew venom, some made sense...
Irrespective of intention, the existence stayed tense...
Thoughtless charade long lost its essence...
All lost except the Kasher perseverance...

Carpet-baggers and parasites of the day...
Sought power, wealth, and made hay...
Some sang the anthem, a few still said nay...
Lost was the purpose, lost was the way...

The tide stemmed, the flow ebbed...
The idea of normalcy, you held in your stead...
Schools opened and buses did ply...
Tourists came and extended their stay...

The parleys had begun, the strings pulled...
The philanderer imposed, *vox populi* culled...
Amoral was the reign, all vices at play...
Nepotism and corruption, Kasher failed to slay...

Terror, peace, polity, and bearers of pall...
An Old Janus entertained, hobnobbed with all...
Some in Dilli heeded the devious call...
Tried to pave their path for a cherished recall...

A coalition of hope and that of revival...
Cunning and pretensions made everything trivial...
Many promises made, a little progress done...
But peace and reconciliation were not to be the one...

Healing touch and redressal across the board...
Some of the musings did hit a common chord...
A road opened and buses plied across...
Later episodes revealed compulsions gross...

Two decades lost and a hundred thousand dead...
Humanity lost and countless souls shred...
Chanakya and Machiavelli plotted and schemed again...
Sold their souls to devil to perpetuate their reign...

Moronic philanderer was a jester...
Some affection he'd occasionally muster...
The cub turned out to be a clown...
Killed and maimed to save his crown...

Clampdown here and shutdown there...
Shootout here and letdown there...
Backout here and handsdown there...
Meltdown here and writedown there...

Hollow rhetoric and pointless candour...
Roadside banter revealed deep seated rancour,
Unwilling to pander, you gathered the clangour...
The cub was booed away in disappointment and anger...

For the Old Janus it was pay dirt…
Mollified masses to encash the hurt…
The hustings proved a positive spurt…
Behind the facade were deliberations covert…

Then came the volte-face…
Unexpected, loaded with farce…
Desperate aspirations he did denigrate…
Made a pact with evil-incarnate…

Shocked and stifled, unable to comprehend…
There was no justification, nothing to defend…
Development, justice, peace and assimilation…
Alas! A poor barter loaded with deception…

370… abrogation, abnegation, dilution, and subjugation…
Indignation, desperation, confrontation, and conflagration…
Fishing in troubled waters never proved a viable proposition…
The manifestation primed as a concerted dispensation…

Divine recall to answer moral depredation…
Old Janus disappeared in the final renunciation…
Whispers and intrigue, analysis, and hope…
Medusa did a checkmate, left no scope…

Storms were gathering, waiting for a crackle…
The twigs were dry, a spark to unshackle…
Medusa failed to haggle, conflicting options left to straddle…
The dignity lost and primed the barrel…

A new generation, a reinforced fervour…
Baptized in terror, an interminable vigour…
Ordained in suffering, motivated by rigour…
Unflinching in faith, resolute in temper…

Out on the roads, out in the fields,
On the rooftops, across the streets,
Across every city, in every town,
Across villages, in vales of renown…

They cry for freedom, they shout for emancipation…
They decry injustice, they condemn decimation…
They abhor duplicity, they villify indignation…
They revile barbarism, they execrate capitulation…

Medusa unnerved, started spewing venom…
Tear gas and bullets, lead pumped in the duodenum…
Slingshots answered and bricks too in continuum…
Alas! The pellets guns didn't comply with a humane interregnum…

Shot in the head, shot in the face…
Shot across the body, shot to efface…
Shot to erase, shot to deface…
Shot as a *coup-de-grace*, a brutal showcase…

Kids, men and women, young and old…
A hundred odd dead, the records told…
A couple of hundred blinded, a few thousand maimed…
Many more in the cage, a few scores damned…

Dilli remained silent, opposition made some noise…
Resistance dubbed rudderless, helpless for a unified voice…
Medusa clueless, doled out strictures in apologetic guise…
Fell for Hobson's choice, helped the Brotherhood rejoice…

The Brotherhood grabbed the resurrection…
The Mlecchas sensed an opportunity for redemption…
Dictates and the Calendar promised revitalization…
Oblivious to the pain and suffering or resuscitation…

Curfews clamped and hartals again prescribed...

Livelihoods withered and life stalled...

Young men hounded and the innocent brutalized...

Futures marred and the present curtailed...

The Kashur traumatized and you stand ravaged...

The deaths reduced to statistics and the suffering ridiculed...

The loss unaccounted for and the pain ignored...

The injustice embedded and the barbarity endorsed...

The destruction incomprehensible and degradation sanctified ...

The hope withered and optimism battered...

But,

Resilience is rewarded and fortitude can be regained...

Faith perpetually reinforced and forbearance can be reaffirmed...

When did it begin?

When shall it end?

Who killed Kasheer?

TWINS OF FATE

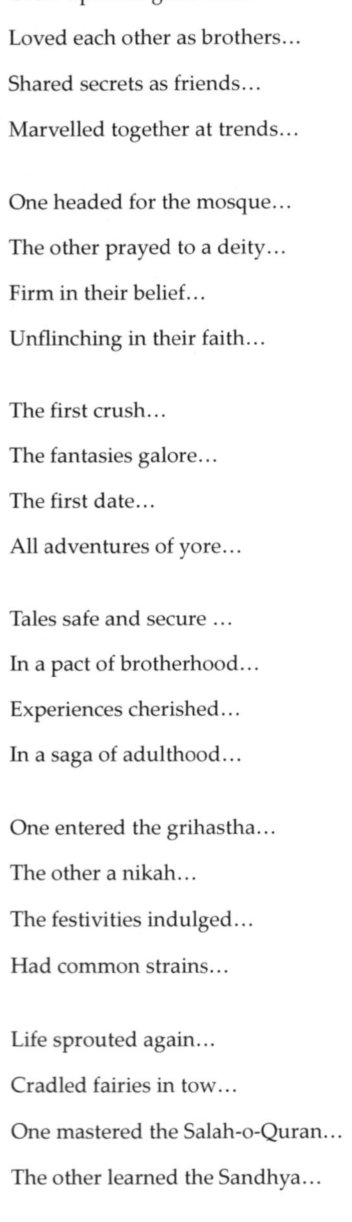

Grew up as neighbours…
Loved each other as brothers…
Shared secrets as friends…
Marvelled together at trends…

One headed for the mosque…
The other prayed to a deity…
Firm in their belief…
Unflinching in their faith…

The first crush…
The fantasies galore…
The first date…
All adventures of yore…

Tales safe and secure …
In a pact of brotherhood…
Experiences cherished…
In a saga of adulthood…

One entered the grihastha…
The other a nikah…
The festivities indulged…
Had common strains…

Life sprouted again…
Cradled fairies in tow…
One mastered the Salah-o-Quran…
The other learned the Sandhya…

Crammed similar rhymes…
Dressed up dolls and toys…
Birthdays celebrated…
On the same day too…

Grew up as maidens…
Well groomed and beautiful…
Steeped in their culture…
Blessed with an intellect bountiful…

Under the starry skies…
On bright summer days…
Looking at dark morose clouds…
On chilly winter days…

In the cherry blossoms…
Under the shade of chinars…
Surrounded by blooms…
On a carpet of leaves…

Wading across rivulets,
Chilling their soles in streams,
Huddling around an autumn fire…
Snuggled cozily in a snowy night…

Haggling together with hawkers…
Shaming the endless gawkers…
Bunking college for a movie…
Or relishing a shopping spree…

They dreamt their dreams…
Scripted their visions…
Whispered their fantasies…
And shaped their lives…

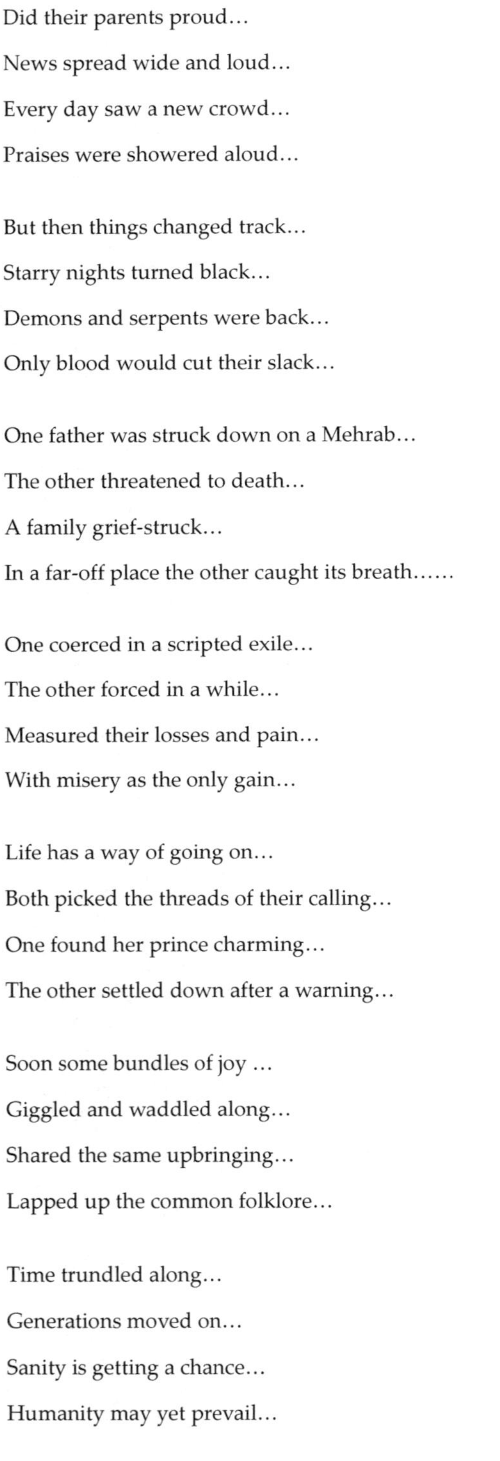

Did their parents proud…
News spread wide and loud…
Every day saw a new crowd…
Praises were showered aloud…

But then things changed track…
Starry nights turned black…
Demons and serpents were back…
Only blood would cut their slack…

One father was struck down on a Mehrab…
The other threatened to death…
A family grief-struck…
In a far-off place the other caught its breath……

One coerced in a scripted exile…
The other forced in a while…
Measured their losses and pain…
With misery as the only gain…

Life has a way of going on…
Both picked the threads of their calling…
One found her prince charming…
The other settled down after a warning…

Soon some bundles of joy …
Giggled and waddled along…
Shared the same upbringing…
Lapped up the common folklore…

Time trundled along…
Generations moved on…
Sanity is getting a chance…
Humanity may yet prevail…

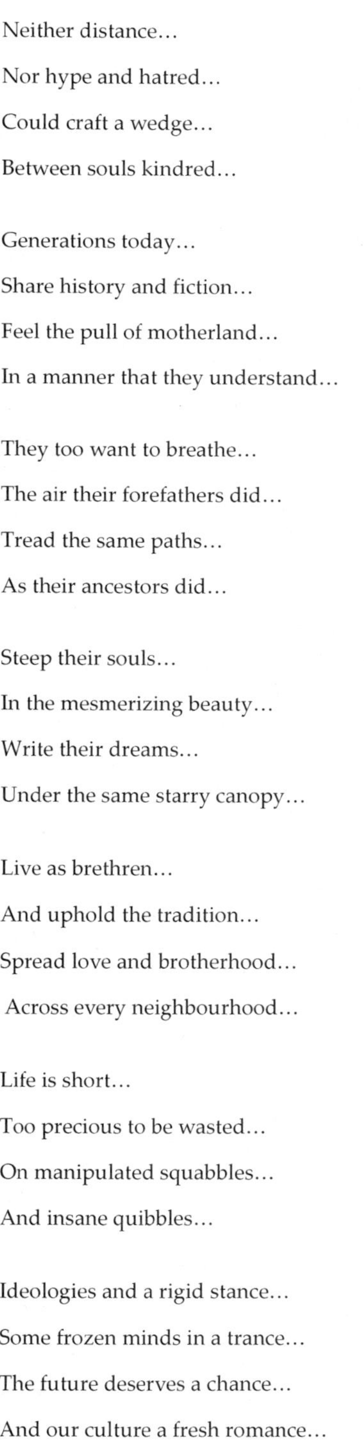

Neither distance…
Nor hype and hatred…
Could craft a wedge…
Between souls kindred…

Generations today…
Share history and fiction…
Feel the pull of motherland…
In a manner that they understand…

They too want to breathe…
The air their forefathers did…
Tread the same paths…
As their ancestors did…

Steep their souls…
In the mesmerizing beauty…
Write their dreams…
Under the same starry canopy…

Live as brethren…
And uphold the tradition…
Spread love and brotherhood…
Across every neighbourhood…

Life is short…
Too precious to be wasted…
On manipulated squabbles…
And insane quibbles…

Ideologies and a rigid stance…
Some frozen minds in a trance…
The future deserves a chance…
And our culture a fresh romance…

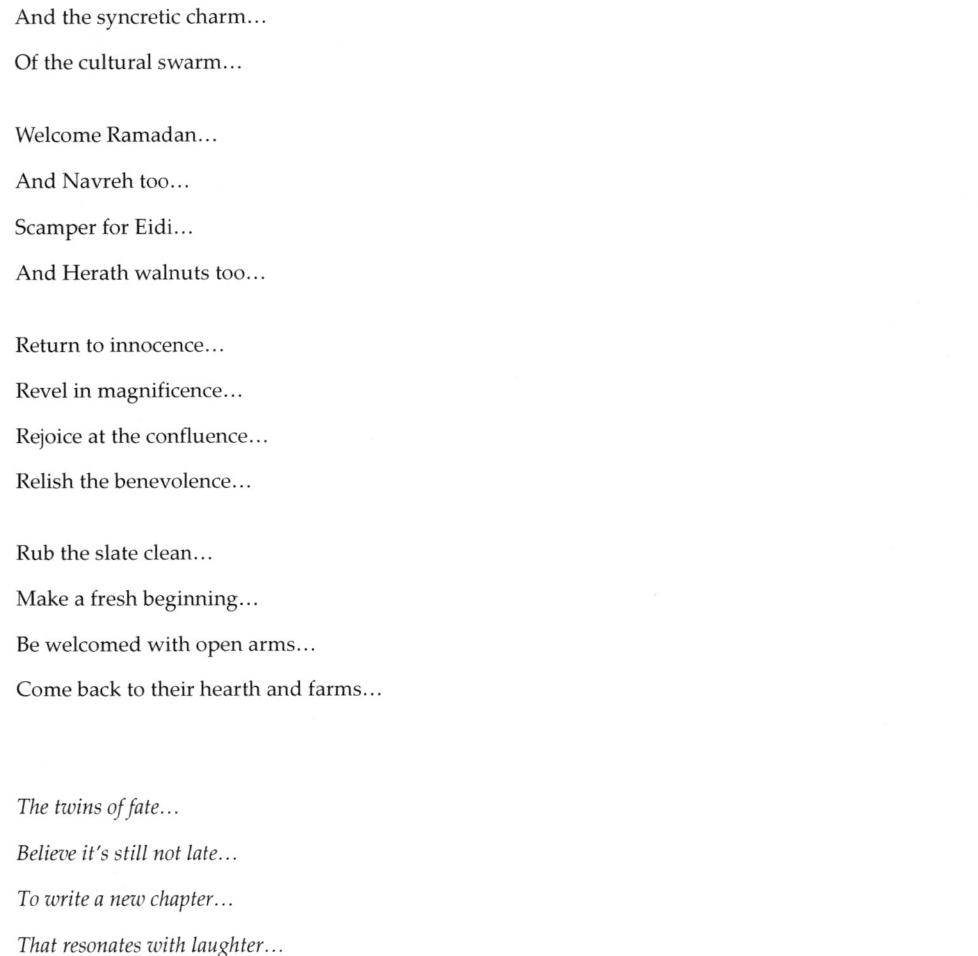

Need to bring the smiles back...

Hugs and kisses too...

And the syncretic charm...

Of the cultural swarm...

Welcome Ramadan...

And Navreh too...

Scamper for Eidi...

And Herath walnuts too...

Return to innocence...

Revel in magnificence...

Rejoice at the confluence...

Relish the benevolence...

Rub the slate clean...

Make a fresh beginning...

Be welcomed with open arms...

Come back to their hearth and farms...

The twins of fate...

Believe it's still not late...

To write a new chapter...

That resonates with laughter...

KASHMIRIYAT

A convoluted truth…
A distorted myth…
A startling reality…
A reason to exist…

A lofty ideal…
A state of being…
A coveted desire…
A cherished dream…

A withered ideology…
A defunct philosophy…
A political expediency…
A religious inclusivity…

A belittled scheme…
A bruised premise…
A broken promise…
A cautious veneer…

A fertile imagination…
A curtailed expression…
A veritable temptation…
A restricted exposition…

A realistic utopia…
A sustainable idea…
A credible panacea…
A tangible exotica…

A raw tragedy…
A viable legacy…
A select fallacy…
A random policy …

A plausible option…
A syncretic notion…
A ridiculed proposition…
A glorified justification…

A perpetual bond…
A dignified stand…
A moral stance…
A timeless practice…

A refuge for sanity…
A haven for diversity…
A sanctuary for humanity…
A retreat for magnanimity…

An exploited theme…

CRACKDOWN!

The fairyland swathed with a virgin carpet of snow…
And the subjects dreaming about a better tomorrow…
The lives ballads of pain and never ending sorrow…

The trolls of misery have blocked every way…
And the werewolves of fear hold their sway…
The black dogs of night don't offer any leeway…

The cocks start crowing in haste before the first ray…
And the birds flutter away in fear and abject dismay…
The flocks scared about the portends of the coming day…

The chariots of death begin to line up and array…
And the shape-shifters ready to whip and flay…
The centaurs primed to make some innocents pay…

The ogres sound their bugles to herald the hunt…
And the dwarves rush to the mosques with a grunt…
The elves stand to guard exits in this morbid stunt…

The trumpet of fear is blown from the minarets…
And citizens file out like gnomes and crickets…
The story repeated across cities, towns, and hamlets…

The folks have said their goodbyes and farewells…
And kissed their babies wet like cold winter bells…
The mothers, wives, and sisters retreat to their shells…

The freezing cold gives in to their blushes and sweat…
And some have already visualized their epithet…
The crowd is led to a space across bush and thicket…

The folks feel the frigid snow under their feet of clay…
And wonder who'll lie buried deep by the end of their stay…
The anxious faces, trembling limbs a sad giveaway…

The bogles lead the men, one after the other…
And the elderly appear stoic while young ones shiver…
The males stand before a chariot ready to die or wither…

The cyclops grudgingly waves some lucky ones away…
And the ones marked are whisked roughly straightaway…
The vampires have their hearts fill in this bloody foray…

The arrows of lead pierce the hearts of the innocent…
And the wendigos show no signs of being reticent…
The goblins of death laugh in glee and contentment…

The macabre ritual of fear continues from dawn till dusk…
And one by one souls are sniffed out by the basilisk…
The gravestones shall be hewn as shall the obelisk…

The leprechauns forage for gold in the hearths…
And the satyrs ogle and grope the pure wreaths…
The grim reaper is flush with death and sheaths…

The valkyries are unseen but the boatmen in abundance…
And the air reeked with anger, hate, and repugnance…
The cruelty meted out has to answer divine provenance…

The blood thirst sated and the bolts of pain inflicted…
And the spectacle of barbarity vainly showcased…
The tribe of death and pain scampers away unscathed…

The scarred souls walk, trundle, crawl, or run back home…
And tearful eyes, barely managed smiles are their welcome…
The ordeal unending for those whose deaths were gruesome…

The wailing and heart-wrenching cries pierce the night...
And the shock, grief, and resignation announce the blight...
The lives of parents, siblings, and kids altered overnight...

The night never ending and the wait almost interminable...
And justifications and logic proffered appear unreasonable...
The fatigued minds and the tired bodies rightly inconsolable...

The bodies arrive; scarred, tortured, and some even disfigured...
And the redolence of myrrh and musk appears to be sacred...
The last look, the last kiss, and embrace forever treasured...

The calls for vendetta, cries of anger, and pent up frustration...
And the hollow professions of the polity aiding the alienation...
The futility of protests and the idea of justice an aberration...

The helplessness writ large on every sad and distraught face...
And the brains teased and souls wracked for a saving grace...
The denouement is anything but the annihilation of a race...

What has been achieved so far?
What has been lost till date?

OH! DAUGHTERS OF EVE

Oh! Daughters of Eve…

To those who seek to entrap you…

Tell them…

Your dreams are ignited by passion,

Your synapses are on fire…

With imagination running riot,

Like a canvass by Michelangelo in its splendour…

Your visions beyond the horizon,

Impossibility reined in…

A niche yet to be carved,

Like a justification for the pain of being…

Your truth has been stumbled upon,

By serendipity at play…

Your logic and protestations,

Like pearls marooned in hollow precepts of beliefs…

Your wings clipped short,

Like an earlier mutilation…

And a descent in despondency,

Like Satan shackled in the pit for millennia…

Tears welling up in your eyes,

A storm about to unleash hell…

A defiant one strolling down your cheek,

Like a dew drop caressing a luscious petal…

Stifled desires crash within your bosom,
Smouldering magma seeking a way out…
Words aborted before birth,
Like butterflies trapped within the chrysalis…

Your resistance stands overwhelmed,
As struggling ambers in a dying fire…
And hope petering out,
Like icicles melting to their slow death...

There are glimmers of hope,
And rainbows in the sky…
Days of reckoning beckon ahead,
Like buds frozen in winter thawing to life…

Oh! Daughters of Eve…

To those who belittle you…
Tell them…

You were created as an equal,
as Hawa[PBUH] with Adam[PBUH]…
Civilization has been unjust to you,
as a forgotten chapter in human history…

You are Aasiyah[PBUH],
the Pharaoh's wife…
Steadfast in her faith,
she stood up to the Pharaoh…

Saw a glimpse of her abode,
in the heaven above…
Her soul freed by Allah[SWT],
before she was crushed by a boulder…

You are Maryam[PBUH],
the mother of Isa[PBUH]…
Who was breathed a spirit into her,
by Allah's[SWT's] will…

Anxious and afraid,
she never wavered in her faith…
Her chastity validated,
when Isa[PBUH] spoke from the cradle…

You are Khadijah[PBUH],
the beloved Prophet's[SAW] wife…
Who believed in him[PBUH,]
when nobody else did…

Comforted him[SAW,]
and shared his[SAW] hardships…
Her selflessness earned her[PBUH,]
His[SAW] respect and love above everyone else…

You are Fatimah[PBUH],
the beloved daughter of the Prophet[SAW]…
Wife to Ali[PBUH],
and mother to Hassan[PBUH] and Hussain[PBUH]…

An epitome of fidelity,
and a paragon of generosity and piety…
Her noble disposition,
an example in benevolence and sacrifice…

You are Ayesha[PBUH],
the beloved Prophet's[SAW] wife...
A repository of knowledge,
and narrator of Hadith...

Championed women's participation,
in social and public life...
Guided the Ummah,
and even led an army in the Battle of the Camel...

You are Umm Salama[PBUH],
the beloved Prophet's[SAW] wife...
Who advised him[SAW] ,
during the treaty of Huddaybiyyah and after...

Lifted his[SAW] spirits,
by advising him[SAW] to tonsure his head and sacrifice cattle...
Earlier thrice recalcitrant,
His[SAW] followers were inspired to follow suit...

You are Zainab[PBUH],
the beloved Prophet's[SAW] grand-daughter...
Who held the "Ahl-e-Bayat" together,
during and after Karbala...

Saved Ali ibn al Hussain[PBUH] at Kufa,
and chastised Yazid at Damascus...
Secured the release of "Ahl-e-Bayat",
and left behind a universal legacy...

You are Nusayba of the Banu Najjar,
and the Prophet's[SAW] companion...
Participated in the Battle of Uhud,
and shielded the Prophet[SAW] from enemies...

Or Khawla bint Al Azwar,
who fought alongside Khalid bin Walid…
Decimated the Byzantines at Yarmuk,
and earned herself a place of pride in history…

You are Nafisa[PBUH],
the great granddaughter of our beloved Prophet[SAW]…
Amongst her students was Imam Shafi'i,
the founder of Shafi'i school of fiqh…

Or Hafsa[PBUH],
daughter of Caliph Umar Ibn Al Khattab[PBUH]…
The first person to be entrusted,
with a copy of the written Qur'an…

Oh! Daughters of Eve…

To those who deny your efflorescence…
Tell them…

You have been Lubna of Cordoba,
palace secretary to two Umayyad Caliphs…
Presided over the Royal library,
a writer, grammarian, poet, and a mathematician par excellence…

Or Mallika al Hurra Alwa, Queen of Yemen,
A poet and historian, designated Hujja by the Caliph…
Expert in religious affairs and hadith,
she sent Ismaili missionaries to India…

You have been Fatima bint Abi Al Qasim,
the most learned woman in Islamic Iberia…
A hafiza, expert in Jurisprudence, mysticism,
and innumerable works on Islam…

Or Fatima Al Fihri,
the founder of the "worlds oldest" university at Fez...
Who established mosques and madrassas too,
and is an answer for all your detractors...

You have been Sayyida al Hurra,
evicted from Granada, ruled Tetouan and later Morocco...
Allied with Heyreddin Barbarossa,
and crushed Spanish power in North Africa and Mediterranean...

Or Pari Khan Khanum,
the Persian princess and arbiter of imperial power...
A poet, well versed in Islamic Sciences and Jurisprudence,
who sacrificed herself for posterity...

You have been Rabia Al Adawwiya,
a slave in southern Iraq, founded the Sufi school of "Divine love"...
Who loved Allah[SAW],
but not out of fear of punishment or desire for reward...

Or Zainab bint Ahmad of Damascus,
who acquired Ijazas in Hadith and jurisprudence...
She taught Ibn Batuta, Al Sulki and Al Dahabi too,
and has her name in the isnads of Ibn Hajar al Asqalani...

You have been Umm Al Darda,
the woman who taught the Caliph, Abdul Malik Ibn Marwan...
Considered superior to all the hadith scholars of the period,
she taught jurisprudence at the mosque...

Or Amra Bint Abdurrahman,
who was a jurist, a judge, and an authority on ahadith...
On whose authority a compilation of ahadith was ordered,
by Caliph Umar bin Abdul Aziz...

You have been Zainab Bint Sulaiman,
a princess of the Abbasid Caliphate...
Who gained an impeccable reputation,
as the finest woman scholar of her time...

Or Shuhaddah Bint Ahmad al Ibrii,
a scholar and jurist of Baghdad...
Studied with male scholars,
and became well-known as the "pride of women" of that era...

You have been Ayesha Bint Sa'ad,
a renowned jurist and scholar of her time...
She was the teacher of Imam Malik,
the founder of Maliki school of Jurisprudence...

Or Sitt-ul-Mulk,
the Fatimid princess from Egypt, who made a mark in public life...
She was admired as an expert in Islamic administration,
by one and all across the realms...

You have been Asifa Bint Abdullah,
a manager and inspector of markets during Caliph Umar's[PBUH]reign...
and Karimah Al Marwazziyah,
who tutored Al Khatib and Al Humaydi on Abu Dharr's recommendation...

Or Fatimah bint Muhammad,
also known as Shahada...
who was titled as "Masnida Asfahan",
Scholars of repute flocked to be her students and master Islamic studies...

You have been Zainab Bint Kamaal,
who taught hundreds of books on Ahadith in institutions across Damascus...
and Dhayfa Khatun, Salahuddin Ayubi's daughter-in-law,
who defeated Seljuks, Mongols, and the crusaders too...

Or Amina, a queen of Zazzua in Nigeria,
who ruled for decades and made vast conquests…
She is credited with developing an intricate system,
a host of defensive stratagems and structures known as Amina's walls…

Oh! Daughters of Eve…

To those who challenge you…
Tell them…

You can be Laleh Bakhtiyar,
the first American woman to translate Quran in English…
Or Shirin Ebadi,
the first Muslim woman to win the Nobel Prize for peace…

And Anousheh Ansari,
the first Muslim woman to make it to space…
Or Cissé Mariam Kaïdama Sidibé,
the first woman prime minister of Mali…

You can be Maryam Mattar,
one of UAE's finest civil servants donning multiple hats…
or Adeeba Kamarulzaman,
of Malaysian Aids Council, the taboo breaker…

and Maryam Mirzakhani,
an esoteric Iranian-American mathematician of global repute…
or Rana Dajani,
the current Arab world's acclaimed and exemplary social innovator…

You can be Sameera Mousa,
the nuclear physicist, who tamed nuclear energy to affordability…
Or Nesreen Ghaddar,
Qatari chair of energy studies, a fellow of Islamic World Academy of Sciences…

And Ismahane Elouafi,
world renowned geneticist and global scientific trail-blazer and leader…
Or Ilham Al Qaradawi,
the nuclear scientist who bought extensive laurels to her nation…

You can be Sania Nishtar,
globally acclaimed cardiologist, activist, author, and politician…
Or Hessa Al Jaber,
engineer, academic, and politician and first women minister in Qatar…

And Hina Chaudhry,
the dynamic cardiac magician every intern wants to emulate…
Or Hayat bint Sulaiman,
a medical scientist and a member of the Saudi Consultative Assembly…

You can be Tansu Ciller,
who is the only woman prime minister of Turkey till date…
Or Meghawati Sukarnoputri or Ameenah Fakim,
ex-presidents of Indonesia and Mauritius…

And Mame Madior Boye or Aminata Toure,
both have been prime ministers of Senegal…
Or Atife Jahjaga, the president of Kosovo;
the youngest in the world till date…

Oh! Daughters of Eve…

To those amongst you who dither and dally…
Tell them…

All that is needed is a peep into the past,
Of glorious times gone by with no bias or prejudice…
When women were embodiments of excellence and Intellect,
Looked up to guide and nourish human soul and mind…

Redemption was always within your ambit,
It's embedded within your soul…
Nothing has been placed beyond your reach,
Like a bird in dauntless flight…

Go out, reach for the stars and fulfill your destiny…
May Allah[SWT] be with you…
Amen!

PRECOCIOUS BUDS

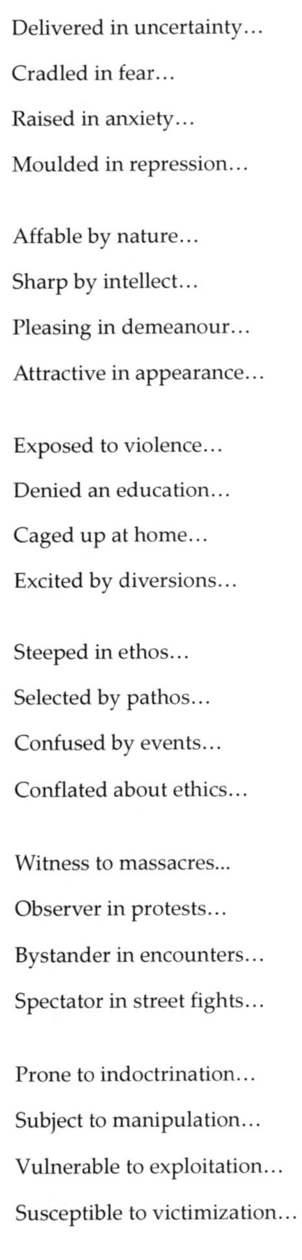

Delivered in uncertainty…
Cradled in fear…
Raised in anxiety…
Moulded in repression…

Affable by nature…
Sharp by intellect…
Pleasing in demeanour…
Attractive in appearance…

Exposed to violence…
Denied an education…
Caged up at home…
Excited by diversions…

Steeped in ethos…
Selected by pathos…
Confused by events…
Conflated about ethics…

Witness to massacres...
Observer in protests…
Bystander in encounters…
Spectator in street fights…

Prone to indoctrination…
Subject to manipulation…
Vulnerable to exploitation…
Susceptible to victimization…

Pampered with affection…
Cajoled with reasoning…
Manoeuvred with care…
Persuaded with facts…

Shielded from the devil…
Ogled by the evil…
Secured from peril…
Groomed to be civil…

Days turn into weeks…
And weeks into months…
Seasons give way…
And the skies change too…

Unsure about the present…
Uncertain about the future…
Cloistered in opportunities…
Cluttered with possibilities

Realities surface…
Resolve hardens…
Reasoning evolves…
Recriminations increase…

The buds are at the crossroads…
The buds need to be inspired…
The buds need to be understood…
The buds need to be given a chance...

Precocious they are…

SAD FLOWS THE JHELUM

Oh! Jhelum...
Blessed you were with life since antiquity...
Destined you are to flow till eternity...

You were called Hydaspes by Greeks...
Vedas mention you as Vitasta...
Kasher love you as Vyeth...

You got eulogized as Titan's descendant by Nonnus...
One mythical destroyer named his consort as such...
Dara -e-Azam fixed his flag at Ja-e-Alam hence the name...

You begin your journey from an enchanted spring...
Meander your way through harsh outcrops and lush fields...
Larger and lesser ones merge with you till your journey ends in sea...

You birthed civilizations for millennia on end...
Cradled cultures since times immemorial...
Sustained lives across endless epochs of history...

You witnessed invaders and conquerors across ages...
Battles and ambushes across days and nights...
Banks trodden and waters bloodied over centuries...

You welcomed all across caste and creed, colour, or origin...
Greeks, Huns, Kushans, Mughals, Afghans, Sikhs, and Dogras...
Saw them thrive, leave their mark and vanish with the passage of time...

You saw kingdoms fall and empires rise upon each other's ashes...
Confluence of cultures, intermixing of races, and ascendancy of faith...
Adoption of customs, languages introduced, and taboos shattered...

You watered the fields and drenched countless farms since aeons...
Across epochs fed the gardens and enlivened the blossoms...
Ripened the fruit laden orchards and nourished the Chinars and poplars...

You filled the lakes and ponds and engorged the springs...
Led the waterfalls to their abysmal death and resurrection too...
Overran vast plateaus and plains and hurtled through gorges ...

You carried water that was pure and filled with life and succour...
Healing all maladies and treating malaises like a divine elixir...
Quenching the thirst of masses and offering livelihoods as well...

You marvelled at the childhood playing on your endless banks...
Delighted at the gossip mills churned by the women on your ghats...
Cherished the manhood swimming against the current as a rite of passage...

You blinked in disbelief at the hunched old backs manoeuvring the heavy boats...
Rejoiced at the shikarawallahs ferrying the kids, men, and women across your banks...
Felt at peace with the angler trying to hook fish in your bountiful waters...

You had your colour change from lucid hues in spring to muddy browns in autumn...
Chilly winds arising from your bosom announced the onset of grim winter...
Fragrant invigorating breezes heralded the arrival of much prayed for spring...

You had maharajahs and marriage parties parading down your length in ornamental boats...
Swelled with pride as boats laden with grain and vegetables labored incessantly...
Giggled in pleasure at the sight of kids trying to catch up with tourists in the Shikaras...

You had never imagined that such days of bliss shall be swallowed by evil ones to come...
Though you had borne the sight of putrid bodies of hanged natives dangling from your bridges...
But what was to come your way would shrink and slow you down into oblivion...

You bore the sight of lands you watered pillaged in punishment...
Folks you had sustained tortured, maimed, and killed in admonishment...
Communities you provided for hounded and stripped of belongings...

You now hear your waters writhe in pain as tied bodies of murdered youth are flung in…
Shudder at the cries of innocents as your frozen waters rob them of their lives forever…
Tremble as you stand in witness to young and old killed in cold blood along your banks…

You quiver in helplessness as women, across all ages, are ravaged and drowned in your womb…
Shiver at the sight of tortured and mutilated bodies fished out in a disturbing consistency…
Convulse in horror as your waters wash ashore decapitated heads and chopped off limbs…

You rue the insanity…
You sigh at the incongruity…
You regret the loss incurred…
You moan at the pain inflicted…
You groan at the suffering imposed…
You bewail the justice denied…
You bemoan the rights trampled…
You deplore the atrocities committed…
You sob at the miseries inflicted…
You cry at the futures sniffed out…
You weep at the dreams cut short…
You ululate at the wounds of hope…
You mourn the loss of innocent lives…
You lament the ravaging of chaste honour…
You grieve the loss of innocence in this murderous melee of violence…

Your Jeremiad is a ballad of suffering…
Your sorrow irreconcilable…
Your pain unendurable…

Sad flows the Jhelum…

TWO SIDES OF A COIN

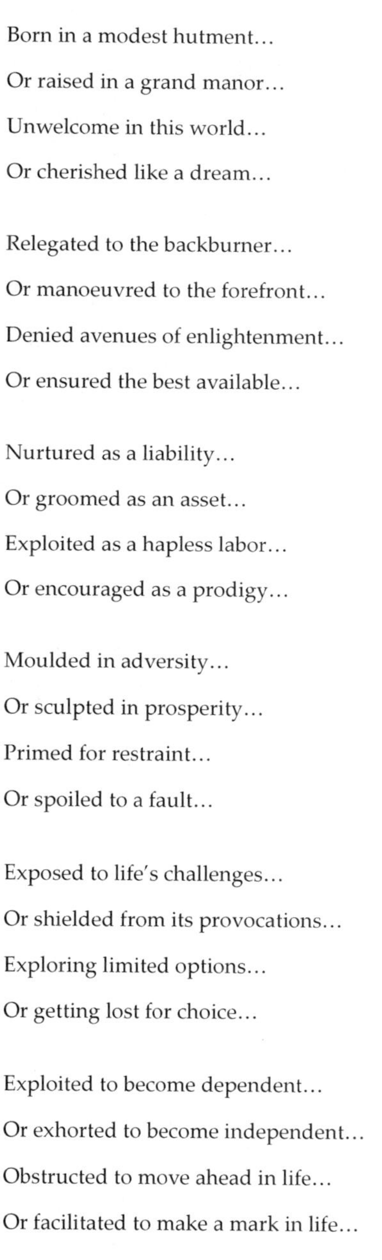

Born in a modest hutment...
Or raised in a grand manor...
Unwelcome in this world...
Or cherished like a dream...

Relegated to the backburner...
Or manoeuvred to the forefront...
Denied avenues of enlightenment...
Or ensured the best available...

Nurtured as a liability...
Or groomed as an asset...
Exploited as a hapless labor...
Or encouraged as a prodigy...

Moulded in adversity...
Or sculpted in prosperity...
Primed for restraint...
Or spoiled to a fault...

Exposed to life's challenges...
Or shielded from its provocations...
Exploring limited options...
Or getting lost for choice...

Exploited to become dependent...
Or exhorted to become independent...
Obstructed to move ahead in life...
Or facilitated to make a mark in life...

Badgered into docile submission…
Or boosted into stiff resistance…
Bludgeoned into discernible obedience…
Or braved into sanctioned rebellion…

Married off as a social compulsion…
Or ensured participation in the decision…
Disposed off without a moral compunction…
Or handed over with due consideration…

Worried about the household rations…
Or indulged in pursuing passions…
Voice smothered in suffocation…
Or a stance taken in liberation…

Burdened with kids at a nascent age…
Or enjoying life's every new page…
Tasked with running home and hearth…
Or reaching out for all she's worth…

Tolerating tempers and demands everyday…
Or being pampered in every which way…
Bearing regular abuse and indignation…
Or hearing praise and commendation…

Considered unequal and inconsequential…
Or treated as equal and considered influential…
Treatment meted out largely circumstantial…
Or indulgences treated as quintessential…

Struggling to cope with the kids' upbringing…
Or dismissing every teenage crush and fling…
Accountable for their career and social grooming…
Or assured of a secure future for her offspring…

Worried about her brood's livelihood...
Or extolled as a paragon of motherhood...
Bearing the pain of a weaned and lonely bosom...
Or being with the flock to enjoy every blossom...

Eager and worried about her nests matrimony...
Or meticulously planning a grand ceremony...
Blamed for familial unrest and acrimony...
Or presented as an icon of peace and harmony...

Carrying on with her life in a ritual of monotony...
Or plotting to ensure her perpetual hegemony...
Contending with erosion of her status and sanctimony...
Or scheming to enforce her writ and testimony...

Braving misery, loss, pain, death, or destruction...
Or globe-trotting from one to another destination...
Thronging dargahs for intercession and supplication...
Or manipulating situations with subtle discretion...

Selfless in an age of fear, uncertainty, and trepidation...
Or focussed on avenues to further her discreet ambition...
Denied justice and harassed even for securing compensation...
Or equally at ease with connections in every dispensation...

Wasted childhood, withered youth, and whimsical old age...
Or living life to the fullest by shaping every stage as an advantage...
Patient by circumstance, penitent by heart with a potent visage...
Or profligate by will, pompous by nature with a proud image...

Limited means douse the eager flame of a cherished desire...
Or flush with riches to wish and acquire all there is to admire...
The pilgrimage to Makkah and Madinah would she aspire...
Or the yearly Umrahs and the occasional Haj that light a fire...

Confined to a decrepit bed in a nondescript government hospital…

Or waited upon by specialists in a super-specialty in the capital…

Bidding farewell to helpless faces is a breeze with a Quranic recital...

Or entangled in wires and tubes peeked at by a crowd so judgmental…

Life comes full circle…

Which path would you dare to tread upon?

Which destination would you crave to reach?

Which journey would you desire to undertake?

SOANTH

Deep below the frigid surface,
frenetic activity is seen apace...
Seeds and bulbs jostle for space,
starved roots haggle and embrace...

With the first thaw in place,
shoots and stems join the race...
To breach the surface in grace,
the first sprouts end this chase...

The gardens come alive with a reface,
countless blossoms thrive face-to-face...
Bumbling bees cease to be a menace,
harvesting nectar on a colourful terrace...

Nervous blades of grass brace,
the chill above and a frozen base...
Narcissus and Lilacs vie for a vase,
Daffodils and Tulips do the landscape lace...

Cherry blossoms set the pace,
palls of gloom they do erase...
Peach, Pear, and Apple blooms lace,
masks of sadness they do efface...

Morose skies disappear without a trace,
though some clouds are hit with a mace...
Erratic showers are never out of place,
feeding gurgling streams loaded with dace...

Snow burdened mountains rid off their grimace,
flush with greenery is the smirk on the staircase…
Melting snow feeds the rivers trying to outpace,
seasonal ones attempting to perennials outrace…

Towering poplars and majestic chinars retrace,
their lost magnificence in a fresh green showcase…
Withered meadows and battered pines resurface,
as lush bounties of nature offering calm and solace…

Graylag geese, Mallards, and Teals repace,
Pochards, Shovelers, and Wigeons leave in grace…
Herons, Egrets, and Lapwings show their face,
Cranes, Hoopoes, and Storks do them outpace…

Hanguls have hibernating bears lose face,
Snow Leopards sometimes deign to aggrace…
Musk Deer, Serows, Marmots, and Weasels unbrace,
Martens, Otters, Hill Foxes, and Jackals relace…

Peasants and farmers tending land are visible everyplace,
hordes of insects crawl out with some hiding behind a carapace…
Folks, rustic and urban alike, prep their gardens in backspace,
saplings planted, weeds pulled out and perennials abrace…

Clew of earthworms and swarms of wasps are seen anyplace,
clouds of gnats and nests of hornets leave their native space…
Kettles of swallows and quarrels of sparrows are commonplace,
convocations of eaglets fly out to leave their birthplace…

Where mountain ridges and saddles interlace,
fresh fires light up the furnace and fireplace…
In the dwellings of the hospitable populace,
the air is evocative of poise and vivace…

Imposing landscapes do engorged rivers enlace,
swelling with pride to deviate and deface...
Hurtling waterfalls, splendid lakes do misplace,
ethereal heaven on earth in such a time and space...

This perennial rebirth does death displace,
the eternal renewal does loss replace...
This perpetual resurrection does life supplace,
the enduring rejuvenation does despair ace...

Hopes are high in a futuristic preface,
dreams are set like gems in a necklace...
Fears are encased in a cautious mindspace,
prayers suffuse every heart with Divine Grace...

Will the Soanth be a harbinger of justice this time?
Or shall it fall in love with history once again?

KASHUR

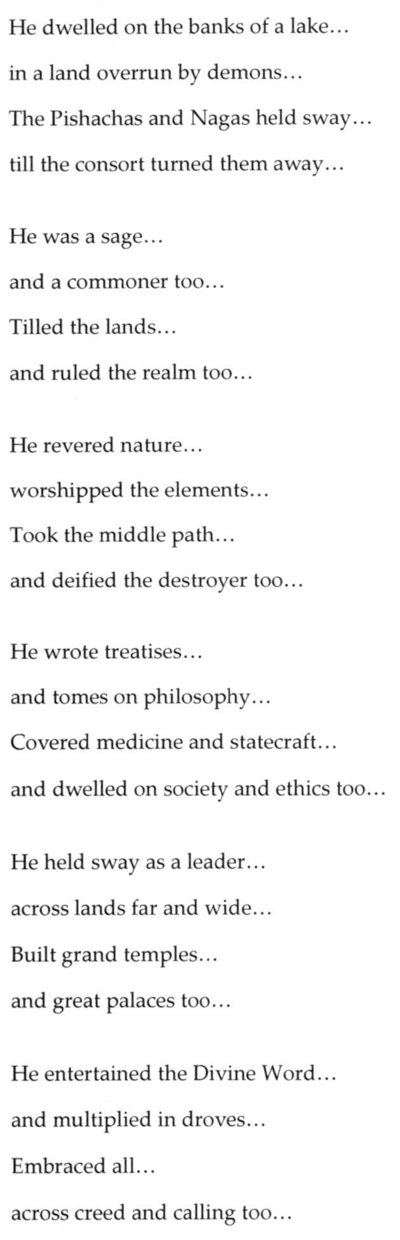

He dwelled on the banks of a lake…
in a land overrun by demons…
The Pishachas and Nagas held sway…
till the consort turned them away…

He was a sage…
and a commoner too…
Tilled the lands…
and ruled the realm too…

He revered nature…
worshipped the elements…
Took the middle path…
and deified the destroyer too…

He wrote treatises…
and tomes on philosophy…
Covered medicine and statecraft…
and dwelled on society and ethics too…

He held sway as a leader…
across lands far and wide…
Built grand temples…
and great palaces too…

He entertained the Divine Word…
and multiplied in droves…
Embraced all…
across creed and calling too…

He adopted a new way of life...
felt enlightened and awake...
Bowed to syncretic influences...
and other thought streams too...

He learned new trades...
enriched the local culture...
Explored and traded...
with outside realms too...

He introduced languages...
wrote epics and poetry...
Scripted masterpieces...
and engaged in research too...

He prospered and blessed...
helped society evolve...
Reached a zenith...
but bore a fall too...

He fought valiantly...
deceit played its part...
Succumbed to a yoke...
and slavery too...

He had his spirit broken...
and honor compromised...
His life snatched...
and dignity too...

One after the other...
the marauders came...
One better others worst...
caused him misery too...

For centuries he endured…
for ages he suffered…
For aeons he bled…
and resisted too…

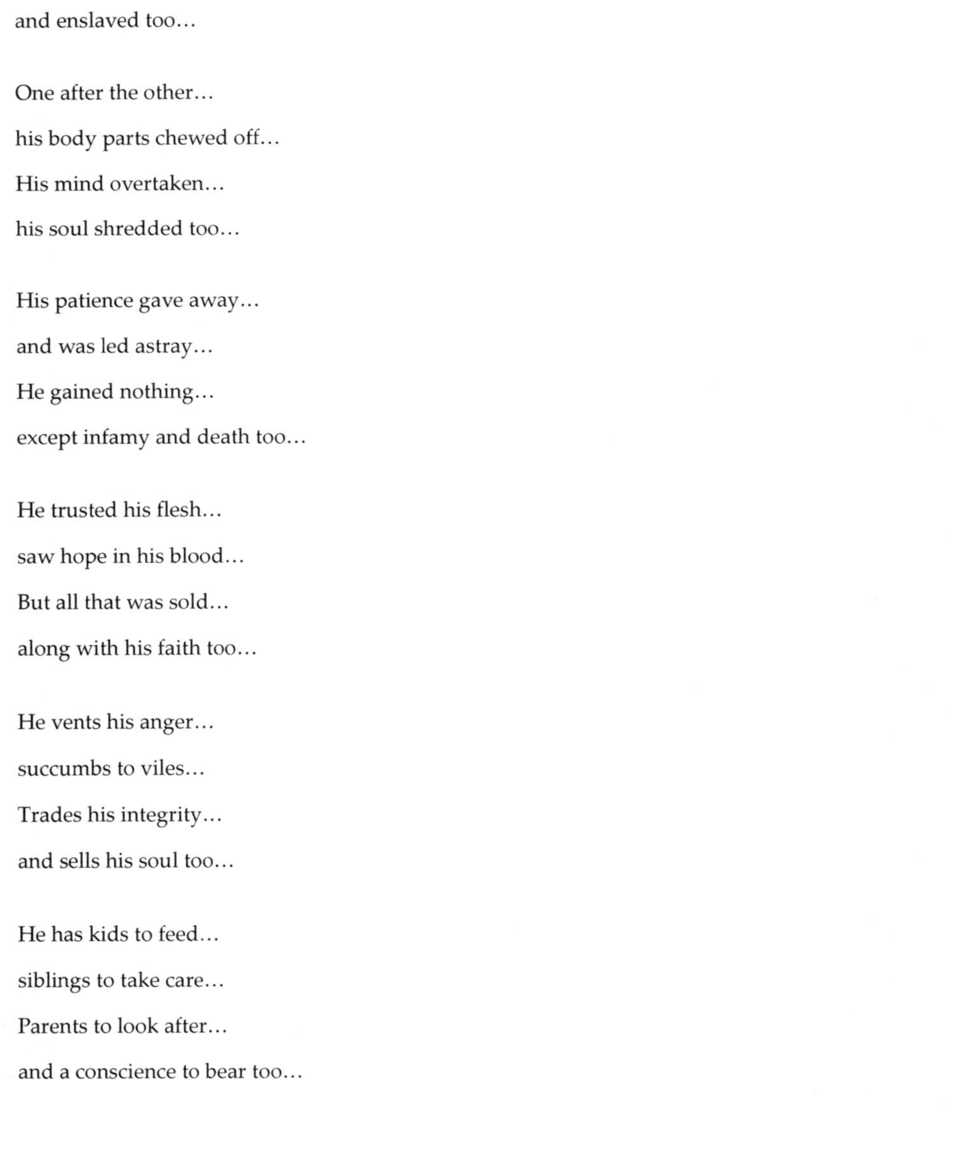

He witnessed relief…
that became temporary…
Once more deceived…
and enslaved too…

One after the other…
his body parts chewed off…
His mind overtaken…
his soul shredded too…

His patience gave away…
and was led astray…
He gained nothing…
except infamy and death too…

He trusted his flesh…
saw hope in his blood…
But all that was sold…
along with his faith too…

He vents his anger…
succumbs to viles…
Trades his integrity…
and sells his soul too…

He has kids to feed…
siblings to take care…
Parents to look after…
and a conscience to bear too…

He clings to every promise...
holds on to every word...
Treasures every sermon...
and follows every direction too...

He still dwells on the banks of a lake...
overflowing with blood...
In the land littered with corpses...
of outsiders and homegrowns too...

Pishachas and Nagas are there again...
causing suffering and immense pain...
There is no one to show him the way...
and no one to turn them away...

He doesn't have a way out...
he doesn't have a way in...
But he has a strong will...
and a stronger faith too...

He is a Kashur...

WHAT IF

Sometimes I wonder…

What if…

Akbar hadn't deceived Yusuf Shah Chak…

Habba Khatoon pined for him and had a sad death…
Uttering priceless nuggets of Lol in her every breath…
Offering countless pearls of solace in a glum wreath…
To women stung by unrequited love across every hearth…

The paradise had its pride shamed in history to dust…
And emblems of a foreign hegemon emblazoned on its crest…
Frequently would the marauders haughtily stride her chest…
And in turn open the gates of opportunity for others to wrest…

The Majestic Mughal gardens in their heavenly countenance…
The ethereal designs with Nature's bounty in abundance…
The mesmerizing ambience overwhelming in attendance…
The liberating experience a showcase of transcendence…

Chashma Shahi with its blessed spring healing since days of yore…
Pari Mahal a secluded haven where Djinns and fairies created folklore…
The majestic Koh-i-Maran capped by a fort as a sentinel to adore…
Pather Masjid a symbol of an empress's piety not used anymore…

Peace in the prestigious realm, a precursor to desired prosperity…
Promotion of local industry across the empire, a show case of creativity…
Inflow of tourists, scholars, and artisans, the enrichment of society…
The paradise on earth, the favourite haunt of Mughal royalty…

The comprehensive initiatives to frame the Revenue settlement...
The improved laws, better governance worked for due betterment...
The bridge of destiny crossed for future political entanglement...
The portend of all things to come with a Divine appointment...

All this would've been just figments of imagination long redundant...

What if ...
The Afghans and later the Sikhs weren't invited...

Inhuman Afghan tyranny wasted the valley for nearly a century...
Destruction of some Mughal gardens, construction of Sher Garhi...
Endless taxation, harsh punishments drove every Muslim to penury...
Brutal murders, mass drowning of Pandits and Shias a sad memory...

Mass migration, burning of fruit trees, suicides committed to escape treachery ...
Innovative means of cruelty, lands made fallow, a remnant of past glory...
Torturing of traders to extort money, a complement of their cruel repertory
The populace withered, every soul terrified in the allegorical purgatory...

The Sikhs, a ruthless and barbaric horde, an odious tenure in the valley's history...
A quarter century of torture, death, rape, and pillage unprecedented and gory...
Daughters defaced and hidden, sons beheaded like flowers plucked in a flurry...
Cow slaughter, call to prayers banned and main mosques closed in a hurry...

Women raped wantonly and abducted for Darbars, an exercise made obligatory...
Licentious governors and vengeful minority, shamed the Afghans in debauchery...
Forced labour and unpayable taxes, shutting of industries an unbearable misery...
Local schools shut down and craftsmen sent outside, acts of a cruel adversary...

All this wouldn't have blunted the pride, honour, economy, and ageless camaraderie...

What if…

The British hadn't defeated the Sikhs…

The Anglo-Sikh wars, the disintegration of Sikh Empire, a Raja's nephew on rise…
Had earlier made some selfish moves, won some battles, got awarded Jammu as a prize…
The Maharaja dead, chaos and disorder in durbar, wanted millions from him for a grouse…
Used his skills to pay a pittance, engaged the British to fraternize and secure his franchise…

The paranoid army wanted him to lead, spurned the offer and didn't refrain to antagonize…
The Sikh campaign went bad and he reached Lahore, offered Primeministership to energize…
He criticized the war, opened duplicitous talks with British, led to Sikh defeat…
The British appreciated his non-involvement and offered an independent kingdom to patronize…

The Treaty of Lahore done, got dismissed by the Darbar as a duplicitous fiend out to aggrandize…
Sikhs offered the British Gulab Singh's domain but they instead maneuvered to legitimize…
Treaty of Amritsar saw the British transfer Kashmir et al to Gulab Singh to rule and terrorize…
He heartily pounced upon by paying 75 lakh Nanakshahi coins, in an opportunity to capitalize …

A successor aided the British in the war of Independence, punished who'd criticize…
Refused shelter to the patriotic mutineers and instead sheltered the British folks to empathize…
Sent a huge complement of his army to aid the British, help them exterminate and brutalize…
Earned British gratitude and a 21-gun salute, to further colonize territories and polarize…

All this wouldn't have clouded our future and dignity had we not been traded as merchandize…

What if…

The Dogras hadn't ruled Kashmir…

Five generations of injustice and barbarity, five generations oppressed and dehumanised…
The darkest chapter in history of the realm, the one hated the most and despised…
New heights of repression and brutality scaled, new depths of inhumanity displayed…
An infamous era of notorious autocrats, an epoch that saw lives and honour trivialized…

Muslims singled out for cruelty with men sent out for unpaid labour, helpless and cowering...
Young maidens kidnapped and ravished, others sent in droves to harem for deflowering...
The soldiers scouring the landscape to pillage resources, leaving the common man grovelling...
Livelihoods and lives snatched with impunity, taxes levied crippling and annihilating...

Cries for freedom suppressed and chastised, leaders jailed and dissenters murdered...
Peaceful protestors massacred, thousands incarcerated and human rights ignored...
The populace awakened and emboldened, spirit of unity and resistance fully restored...
Ethnic cleansing ordered by the Maharaja, the regime's legality and credibility punctured...

The subcontinent liberated and divided, communities butchered and relations eroded...
Political parleys by both sides to secure accession, tribals sent across and towns raided...
The despot preferred Independence over popular sentiment which he summarily discarded...
Standstills had proved ineffective, conditional accession signed and Indian army embedded...

All this wouldn't have mangled our destiny and left the dreams and aspirations degraded...

What if...
Unprincipled, fickle, morally depraved, self-perpetuating villains hadn't been imposed or elected...

Stooges chose sides to rally with, supported the tyrant to lead the emergency administration...
Set up the Dagan Brigade, met the Sardar and exploited popular sentiment and frustration...
Friendships based on deception didn't last long; the stooge was uprooted with an admonition...
Ordered to the dungeon for a decade or so, his throne was occupied by a rival disposition...

The "Architect" reigned during the hiatus, undertook projects catering to populist imagination ...
Protected 370 and resisted its dilution, benefitted the masses and earned due appreciation...
The powers that be didn't like his popularity, schemed to create a new dispensation...
A puppet installed and Moi-e-Muqaddas stolen, to distract people and create confusion...

A different stooge set up for a sinister purpose, the title downgraded to aid occupation...
Elections rigged and popular sentiment stifled, promises scrapped to aid illegal integration...
The third war fought and a nation disintegrated, caged up stooge smelled resurrection...
Sold his soul and a nation's sacrifices, wound up the Plebiscite Front for his restoration...

The lion had shrivelled to a pliant cat, the passion fizzled out in shameful desperation…

Populist measures and vote bank politics, divided the populace in diabolical machination…

One by one the edifice and the pillars eroded, one by one the ideals fell to subjugation...

The popular dreams and aspirations withered, an unalterable course set for emancipation…

All this wouldn't have erased the confidence of the masses and created a powder keg for future conflagration…

What if…

The Pandit migration and Muslim ethnic cleansing hadn't happened…

The stifling of opinion and asphyxiation of freewill, the censure of sanity…

Self-centred politicians and incompetent bureaucrats, the showcase of servility…

Ideological genuflections and kowtowing creed, the smothering of fidelity…

The exclusion of majority and episodes of discrimination, the fissures in fraternity…

The covert initiatives and selective recruitments, the scripting of a Mutiny…

Ideological brainwashing and religious sermonizing, the galvanizing of a Nationality…

Manipulation of truth and distortion of history, the cracks in the credibility…

The free reign of terror and unmitigated misery, the abnegation of human rights in totality…

The extermination of an ethos and exodus of humanity, a failure in civility…

Ethnic intolerance and aggravation of greed, an indelible slur on humanity…

Cultural revisionism and enforcement of alien mores, a grim travesty…

The chilling insensitivity and abetment of deception, a distorted mentality…

The barbaric reprisals and degradation of human dignity, the template of brutality…

Incarceration, torture, disappearance and murder of youth, the pattern of barbarity…

Rapes, kidnappings, molestations, and murder of women, the tool of savagery…

The draconian laws and incessant aberrations of justice, the instrument of inhumanity…

All this wouldn't have transformed the region into a veritable hell…

What if…

BAPTISM

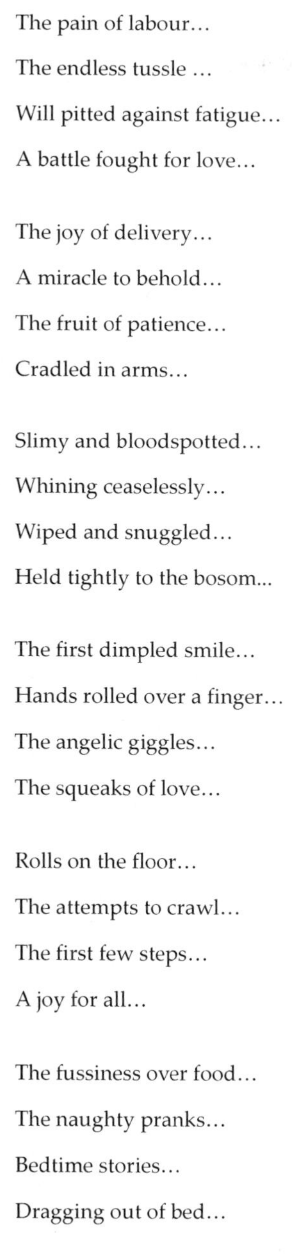

The pain of labour…
The endless tussle …
Will pitted against fatigue…
A battle fought for love…

The joy of delivery…
A miracle to behold…
The fruit of patience…
Cradled in arms…

Slimy and bloodspotted…
Whining ceaselessly…
Wiped and snuggled…
Held tightly to the bosom...

The first dimpled smile…
Hands rolled over a finger…
The angelic giggles…
The squeaks of love…

Rolls on the floor…
The attempts to crawl…
The first few steps…
A joy for all…

The fussiness over food…
The naughty pranks…
Bedtime stories…
Dragging out of bed…

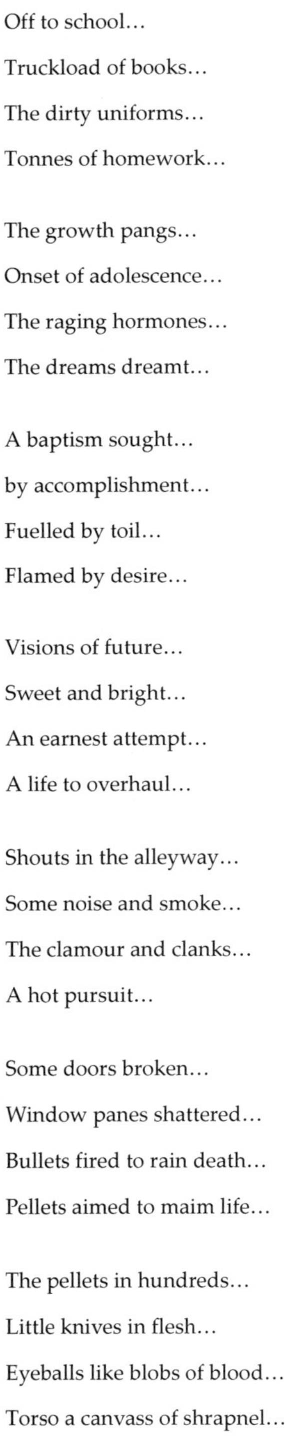

Off to school…
Truckload of books…
The dirty uniforms…
Tonnes of homework…

The growth pangs…
Onset of adolescence…
The raging hormones…
The dreams dreamt…

A baptism sought…
by accomplishment…
Fuelled by toil…
Flamed by desire…

Visions of future…
Sweet and bright…
An earnest attempt…
A life to overhaul…

Shouts in the alleyway…
Some noise and smoke…
The clamour and clanks…
A hot pursuit…

Some doors broken…
Window panes shattered…
Bullets fired to rain death…
Pellets aimed to maim life…

The pellets in hundreds…
Little knives in flesh…
Eyeballs like blobs of blood…
Torso a canvass of shrapnel…

Organs ripped apart…
Blood oozing like miniature rivulets…
Body shivering with cold…
The garbled words…

The throes of mortis…
A lopsided tussle …
Dreams against decimation …
A battle for survival…

The pain of death…
A misery to bear…
The fruit of barbarity…
Lying in arms…

Smeared and blood splattered…
Shrieking in pain…
Wrapped in embrace…
Held tightly to the bosom…

The stammered Shahada…
The last gasps of breath…
A listless body…
The ascent to Jannah…

The baptism happened…
4.5mm they were…
He was all of sixteen…
Too old to live…

KASHER KOOR

You are a paragon of beauty,
The acme of perfection…
An epitome of patience…
The apotheosis of fortitude…

You are a paradigm of innocence,
An ideal of selflessness…
An embodiment of faith…
A personification of sacrifice…

You are the quintessence of love,
A model of fidelity…
An exemplar of accommodation,
An archetype of strength…

You are the standard of resilience,
A champion of mercy…
The beau ideal of compassion,
A friend nonpareil…

You can mould personalities,
Shape the futures of generations…
Enrich the raw minds…
Provide succour to the lost souls…

You can cultivate bonds in a fraternity
Nurture humanity at all times …
Imbibe values to one and all…
Sustain culture across disparate milieus…

You can dream about anything…

From the mundane to the impossible…

Desire anything under the sun…

From the unattainable to the unimaginable…

You can achieve anything…

From the unthinkable to the unachievable…

Overcome anything anywhere …

From the impassable to the insurmountable …

You are a Kasher Koor…

THE CONCH THAT FELL SILENT

Ah! my favourite teachers...
Beacons of vaunted knowledge...
And some of my friendly reapers...
Intellects to live up to a pledge...

Assured sobriety and decency...
Stood out as their hallmarks...
Exemplary erudition and efficiency...
Were hailed as their trademarks...

The camaraderie and brotherhood,
Witnessed largely for a long millennium...
The cultural synergy and neighbourhood,
Terminated by an unexpected interregnum...

They populated the vale in continuum...
Parchment and paddy earned them their livelihood...
Hurried misjudgments led to a sad requiem...
For a community which so tall had for ages stood...

The Saraswat Brahmins were titled Pandits...
As impress they did the Mughal sovereign...
Their intelligence had earned them their plaudits...
And got a benefactor in emperor Akbar...

Earlier on too, BadShah had patronized them...
Sought them for counsel as advisors ...
Called them back from exile and protected them...
Got Rajataragini translated and allowed Dharmashastras...

They prospered with the pen and the produce…
Of serfs and tillers they created an exploited class…
To penury and misery they had them reduce…
Shorn of rights and dignity en masse…

Benevolent rule was overtaken by barbarity…
Neither the landlord nor the serf could escape cruelty…
Birbal Dhar and his son petitioned the Sikh Royalty…
Assured them a province and unflinching fealty…

Soon the Sikhs were masters of the grand realm…
And the Dhars were toasted as society's cream…
They were bestowed grand jagirs by the new regime…
Connived with tyranny to make the serfs scream…

Time sped by as history opened a new chapter…
An obscure Raja got the territory on a cheap platter…
The landlords and traders thought it fit to flatter…
Worked in tandem to inflict misery and see lives shatter…

But there was a genteel crop unbiased and untainted…
That worked hard to alleviate the misery …
Tried to loosen the stranglehold for the unacquainted…
Their efforts and success made others jittery…

Winds of resistance gathered strength and speed…
Oblivious of caste and agnostic of creed…
The last hegemon fled felled by his greed…
The mass movement did ultimately succeed…

While communities elsewhere in fear did cower…
The Pandits felt secure as assurances did shower…
Land settlement changed the balance of power…
Justice was delivered to let prosperity flower…

Some lost their privilege and some their authority…
Some never forgot and wasted lives in insecurity…
But rapprochement was pursued by the majority…
And received well by brethren in the minority…

The past was forgotten and new promises made…
Friendships were forged again never to fade…
Neighbourhoods were abuzz with a lover's serenade…
Feasts were shared that pulled down the ageing barricade…

Haj-i-Baitullah and Milad-ud-Nabi[SAW]…
Navroz, Muharram, and Ramadan…
Urs, Shab-i-Baraat, and Shab-i-Qadr…
Eid-ul-Fitr and Eid-ul-Adha…

Navreh and Herath, Pan and Gaade Batte…
Gengah Atham, Tila Atham, and Huri Atham…
Khetsimavas, Zyeath Atham, and Zarma Satham…
Tiky Tsoram, Vyetha Truvah, and Anta Tsodah…

Observances respected and participation ensured…
The youth volunteered and assistance assured…
Fun and frolic, peace and gaiety were revered…
Tolerance and respect, enriched and matured…

Mosques and Temples existed side by side…
Acrimony and rancour would no longer divide…
The Aadhaan would resonate as a call to abide…
The conch would reverberate as a nod to guide…

Alas, for some latent grudges never did disappear…
And in some deep-seated prejudices were aglare…
Discrimination and denial did many a mind ensnare…
Changing winds laid some old fault lines bare…

Violence and rabble-rousing, intimidation and fear…
Scheming and plotting, devious intentions made clear…
Exhortations and accusations, became unbearable to bear…
Threats and invitations, hid behind a deceptive veneer…

Death was unleashed and so was depredation…
Sanity disappeared and civility slid as an aberration…
Rumours were fuelled by an evil administration…
The brethren succumbed to this political machination…

In open daylight and under the cover of darkness…
They fled in flocks and droves without a harness…
Frustrated and famished they couldn't bear the harshness…
They craved and ached for their dwellings in the fastness…

Some houses occupied and some burnt to an amber…
The leftovers stolen leaving nothing for a progeny to remember…
Some bore a deserted look and some seemed to ponder…
Trying to make sense of the events that had the society dismember…

Leaving behind bungalows and villas, hutments, and ramps…
Young and old, men and women treated like desperate tramps…
Duped and dumped unceremoniously in filthy refugee camps…
Jarred and jam-packed in open dormitories with broken lamps…

The comforts of life, the struggle for a livelihood…
The social prestige, the security of neighbourhood…
The lost childhood, the escapades of adulthood…
The burden of falsehood, the reasons misunderstood…

A new beginning, a fresh struggle to survive…
Denial and acceptance, a renewed impetus to thrive…
An indefatigable will, a lit-up spirit in overdrive…
The instinct to prevail, a diaspora no one can deprive…

Back home…

The temples stood abandoned, the bells stopped ringing…

The sanctums were deserted, the priests stopped chanting…

The gates stood unmanned, the cymbals stopped clanging…

The adherents were absent, the hymns stopped reverberating…

The conch that fell silent…

Is still there…

Waiting…

For you…

SANGBAAZ

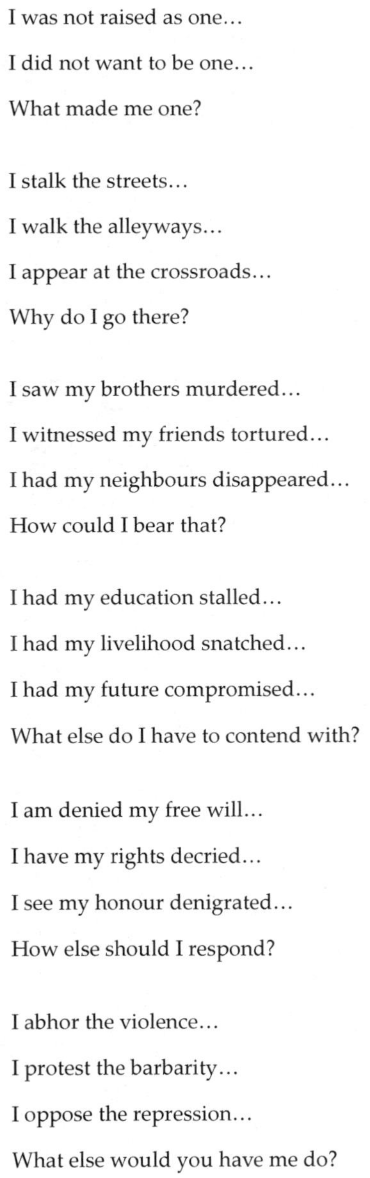

I was not born one…
I was not raised as one…
I did not want to be one…
What made me one?

I stalk the streets…
I walk the alleyways…
I appear at the crossroads…
Why do I go there?

I saw my brothers murdered…
I witnessed my friends tortured…
I had my neighbours disappeared…
How could I bear that?

I had my education stalled…
I had my livelihood snatched…
I had my future compromised…
What else do I have to contend with?

I am denied my free will…
I have my rights decried…
I see my honour denigrated…
How else should I respond?

I abhor the violence…
I protest the barbarity…
I oppose the repression…
What else would you have me do?

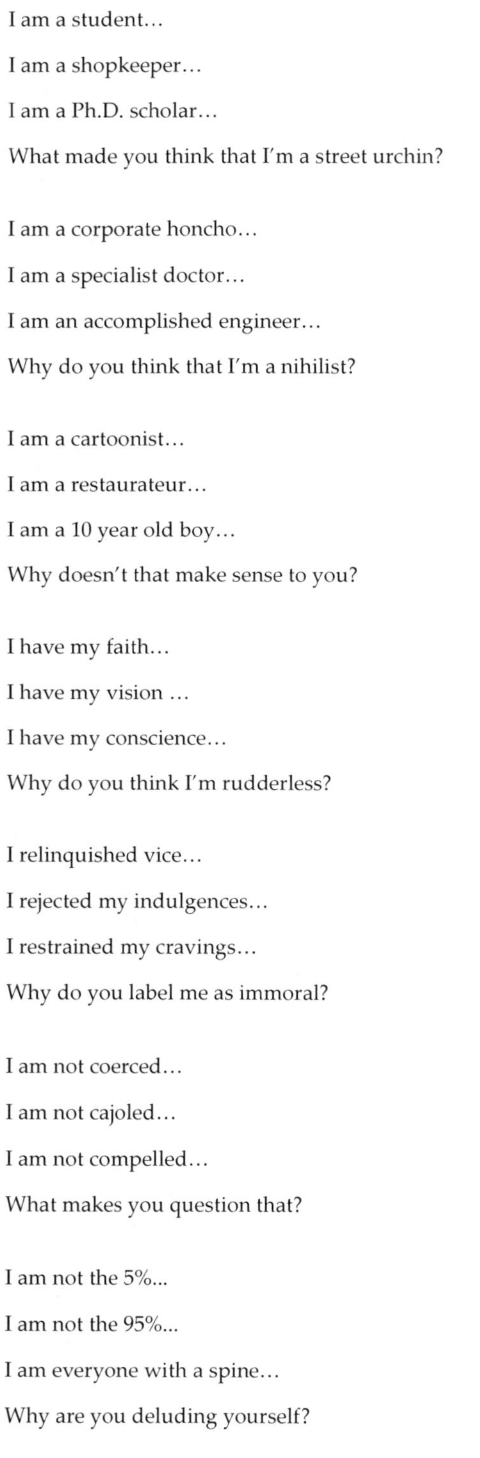

I am a student...
I am a shopkeeper...
I am a Ph.D. scholar...
What made you think that I'm a street urchin?

I am a corporate honcho...
I am a specialist doctor...
I am an accomplished engineer...
Why do you think that I'm a nihilist?

I am a cartoonist...
I am a restaurateur...
I am a 10 year old boy...
Why doesn't that make sense to you?

I have my faith...
I have my vision ...
I have my conscience...
Why do you think I'm rudderless?

I relinquished vice...
I rejected my indulgences...
I restrained my cravings...
Why do you label me as immoral?

I am not coerced...
I am not cajoled...
I am not compelled...
What makes you question that?

I am not the 5%...
I am not the 95%...
I am everyone with a spine...
Why are you deluding yourself?

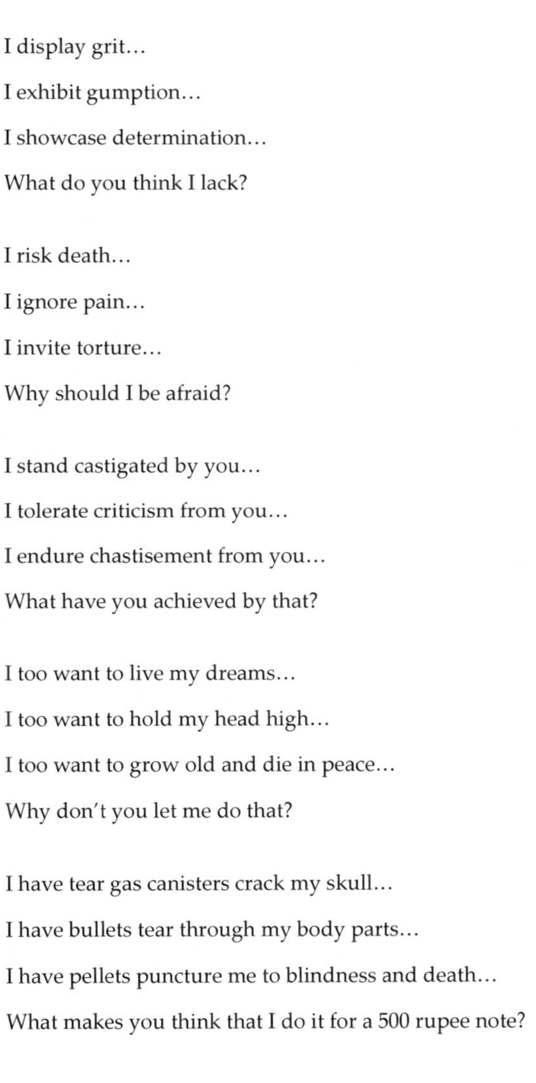

I display grit…

I exhibit gumption…

I showcase determination…

What do you think I lack?

I risk death…

I ignore pain…

I invite torture…

Why should I be afraid?

I stand castigated by you…

I tolerate criticism from you…

I endure chastisement from you…

What have you achieved by that?

I too want to live my dreams…

I too want to hold my head high…

I too want to grow old and die in peace…

Why don't you let me do that?

I have tear gas canisters crack my skull…

I have bullets tear through my body parts…

I have pellets puncture me to blindness and death…

What makes you think that I do it for a 500 rupee note?

TIME

Time we adopt faith and shirk disbelief ...

Time we relish humility and deflate egos...

Time we decide and question insouciance...

Time we embrace courage and banish fear...

Time we accept truth and shun falsehoods...

Time we accept peace and abhor squabbles...

Time we embrace all and excoriate exclusion...

Time we respect dissent and bury impositions...

Time we salvage honour and decimate affronts...

Time we demand justice and overthrow tyranny...

Time we craft a legacy and relinquish ignominy...

Time we promote brotherhood and ignore discord...

Time we materialize dreams and fracture fantasies...

Time we believe in ourselves and stifle incredulity...

Time we seek knowledge and discourage ignorance...

Time we welcome redemption and reject temptations...

Time we stand tall and proud and expel inconsequence...

Time we are ONE...

Amen!

HOPE AND BEYOND

I hope to…

Hear the loudspeakers amplify the call to morning prayers…
Not to terrify souls to parade for an uncertain future…
See the guns silenced and pellets banned…
Not used to massacre and maim the masses…

Relish the sight of the common man setting out fearlessly…
Not folks venturing out only after reciting the shahada…
Bless boys and girls out in droves to secure an education…
Not to see them denied that by burnt and occupied campuses…

Encourage the youth witnessing their dreams take flight…
Not their souls departing without saying good byes…
Cherish the elderly huddling together to discuss politics…
Not harassed and harried as threats to security…

Imagine brides and grooms reaching their homes safely…
Not being murdered or ravaged along the way with impunity…
Chance upon couples pledging love in the moonlit saffron fields…
Not witness tortured bodies dumped after surreptitious executions…

Amble through the tortuous bylanes and streets of cities and towns…
Not get bundled in an unmarked vehicle never to be seen again…
Laze through the pleasant summers on the deck of a houseboat…
Not float as a bloated corpse after a waterboarding gone wrong…

Shed tears of joy upon the return of innocence to the rosy cheeks of cherubs…
Not tears of helplessness to see their families get butchered…
Enjoy the smile on every face and tears exiled till eternity…
Not a pall of gloom as a curse in perpetuity…

Have love, respect, dignity, and happiness cherished as perpetual companions…
Not death, loss, pain, and suffering as one…
Conjure an ethos where wails of pain and shrieks of fright are banished forever…
Not the one that chokes giggles and laughter to inconsequence…

Witness nights of contentment lull everyone to sleep…
Not nights of terror and macabre nightmares…
Imagine people opening their doors with a smile to welcome all…
Not cower in fear with a knock on their doors…

Spot kids straining their eyes in a vain attempt to count birds in flight…
Not running for cover under a barrage of gunfire…
Visualize open spaces being used as playgrounds for tiny tots…
Not hurriedly converted cemeteries reeling under the weight of dreams cut short…

Be amongst the boys and men swimming across the majestic Jhelum…
Not jumping to save myself from bricks thrown and pellets fired…
Experience inclusivity, religious tolerance, and camaraderie…
Not lies, fabrications, distortions, and falsehoods to divide and deject…

Congratulate fathers as they celebrate their sons mature to adulthood…
Not carry the unbearable burden of their corpses to graves…
Compliment mothers who rejoice as their daughters break taboos in life…
Not live in the ignominy of their ravished honour…

Inspire sons and daughters to return from self-imposed exiles…
Not shun their responsibilities as caretakers of their parents' senescence…
Observe folks begin their days with a fresh purpose…
Not fritter them away in an injudicious waste…

Spot the populace shaken out of its forced slumber...
Not squander their precious lives without any purpose...
Motivate anglers lazily whiling away their time hooking fish...
Not fish unrecognizable bodies out of freezing waters...

Persuade friends of yore to return as neighbors...
Not to hold grudges and bay for each other's blood...
Welcome the time when intellect and meritocracy shall rule the roost...
Not when sycophancy and nepotism stifle talent...

Beam proudly at future generations holding their heads high...
Not pity the ones who freeze or overreact at the sight of fatigues...
Be part of families living together with dignity and free will...
Not those coerced into servile submission by alien strains...

Smell the air redolent with the fragrance of enchanting flowers...
Not the one smelling of burnt flesh and charred houses...
Admire the ethereal beauty of myriad perennials...
Not spread them on tombstones of lives terminated abruptly...

Feel the tingling dew massaging my soles to ecstasy...
Not reveal secrets of souls lost in transition...
Witness the cherry blossoms in mesmerizing bloom...
Not their petals speckled with the innocent's blood...

Follow the murmurations of the birds criss-crossing the heavens...
Not in confused darts zipping away from deafening explosions...
Track the comets racing across the dazzling night skies...
Not the trails of tracers and the flares fired to spot and kill...

Trek through the mountain fastnesses to attain solitude…
Not tagged as an intruder and killed in cold blood…
Dip and numb my calves in the cold springs and ponds…
Not stumble upon a decapitated head long rotten…

Admire the Chinars ablaze in their withering majesty…
Not mirror the mangled mortals splattered with dried crimson…
Enjoy the snowflakes dancing and covering the realm like a chaste drape…
Not a mushy shroud stained with rivulets of blood…

I hope to…

YOUP

The overcast skies had taken a dark, melancholic hue…
And the winds betrayed a sad augury as if on a cue…
A few drops trickled down and soon a drizzle did ensue…
And the ferocity of the downpour didn't portend a clue…

The waters crashed down the steep gorges and crevasses…
And the currents engulfed the valleys, plateaus, and meadows…
The streams beamed with pride as they became serpents of fury…
And the ones already there swelled and meandered ferociously…

The mighty waters were on a rampage to herald a divine message…
And the Sodoms of sin and Gomorrahs of evil needed a new visage…
The justice delivered and punishment unleashed on the apostates of age…
As nothing was left sacred and nothing deemed sacrosanct to presage…

Too much blood has spilled and too many innocent voices muffled…
But sadly no voices have been heard nor anyone's conscience ruffled…
Immorality and hypocrisy have been entrenched and faith scuttled…
And humility sniffed out, virtue buried, and the absolute truth nulled…

The fury overtook the villages and left no towns to save or spare…
As the pace of marooning was too overwhelming to avert or prepare…
The cities trembled in fear as the rising waters schemed to ensnare…
And apocalyptic pronouncements and warnings began to duly blare…

The farmland filled up for settlements transformed into a quagmire…
And the catchment drainages clogged by greed became a deathly tripwire…
The wetlands shrunk by human exploitation perennially trapped by desire…
The forests logged to extinction let death silently slip away in their ire …

The castles raised and the manors burnished as specimens of greed…
And the luxuries craved and indulgences displayed by a noxious breed…
The time of reckoning for divine retribution came to denounce this creed…
As the unstoppable force of nature primed for decimation was duly freed…

The torrents overran the embankments and tore through the defenses...
And the bazaars of glamour and gilt resembled their ephemeral pretenses...
The roads mirrored the Venetian canals without the appurtenances...
And the trappings of sinful accumulation were seen trundling over fences...

The folks moved up the storeys as the aquatic elements crept up for balance...
And tried to salvage whatever was left usable or precious for future dalliance...
The faithful understood the wrath and made supplications for a due penance...
As the allegory of grains and husk being sliced together fuelled the forbearance...

The entire realm resembled the primordial habitat of the days of yore...
And once again the evil demons had to be drowned in a new folklore...
The pious and the penitent understood that enticing entrapments galore...
And the temptations of the worldly lives have discontentment in store...

The stories of good Samaritans and guardian angels came to the fore...
As humanity rose above petty divisions and differences like never before...
The welcoming arms and open hearts notched up the good deeds score...
As caste, creed, and class ceased to make any sense in this blessed encore...

The masses relegated their personal problems to the backburner in sometime...
And went about rescuing and feeding the needy covered in mud 'n' slime...
The disaster had brought out the best in people without any reason or rhyme...
And amongst this benevolence unfortunately there also arose a specter of crime...

The waters began to recede overtime but the problems did sadly persist...
As the ineptitude of bureaucracy and the duplicity of polity did exist...
The proclamation of aid and relief was a gesture to duly deny and desist...
As the populace shared resources to rise to the occasion and ably resist...

The experience shook many a soul out of their self-inflicted slumber...
And the cries to cherish and conserve nature came forth in ample number...
The perpetually doomed resorted to accusations to savagely dismember...
And returned to their old practices and prejudices to block and encumber...

The folks across the realm began to fit the jigsaw puzzles of their existence...
And stretched their sinews to maintain sanity and thank gracious providence...
The process was slow and cumbersome but was eased out by prudence...
And soon the ruins of the ravaged rose on the edifices of sincere penitence...

The impertinent, impatient, and impenitent sunk to depths of malevolence...
And the apathy of the powers that be was displayed by their truculence...
The common folks had to bury their dignity to eradicate their despondence...
And along the way consistently tackle apathy, impudence, and indolence...

The chastisement, the castigation meted out and the charades staged for evil...
And the egalitarian amnesia of time perpetuated the legacy of the peril...
The façade of honor and dignity was stripped off and recast on social anvil...
And the downtrodden had to face encumbrances to contend and assail...

Time ticks away...
Experiences expose or enrich...
But what takes precedence?
Is it humility, penitence, pride, or impenitence?

WANDE

Autumn slayed as ordained by the forces of nature…

An Esfandiyar destined to die at Rostam's hands…

Overcast, morose, gloomy skies…

A melancholic canvass painted in sorrow…

The sun taken captive and blinded…

Like KayKavus in captivity of Arzhang Div…

Clouds morphed into myriad shapes…

Recalling Div's from Shahnameh…

Mighty mountains bereft of vegetation…

Proud Pishdad's stripped of their Khvarenah…

Chinars laid bare down to their chaste stumps…

Vain Paladins robbed of their armour…

Their once lush canopies of leaves…

Distorted faces of Sudabeh's witches…

Withered trees in endless rows…

Jinxed lovers, Khosrow and Shirin, in pain…

Dried and deformed leaves in piles…

Like the dead ambers of Hushang's fire…

Ravaged gardens and pillaged blossoms…

The enchanted gardens of Turan laid waste…

Butterflies aimlessly wandering amongst dried petals…

As Faranak milking Barmayeh for Fereydun…

Vine tendrils still clinging to hope…

As did Ferigees's curled locks while pleading for Siyavesh's life…

The once lush fields robbed of life…

Noble Siyamak's death at the hands of Ahriman's son…

Majestic rivers meandering silently across…

As the tears of Arnavaz and Sharnaz mourning Jamshid's death…

Soaring waterfalls aching in their nadir…

As Roodabeh's tresses flung down to pull up Zal…

Chilly winds blowing across the realm…

Whispering rumours about Zahhak's cruelty…

Birds migrating in flocks and droves…

Like Humas never to be seen by a human eye…

First sheets of sleet lost in transition…

An advance guard of Afrasiab…

Heavens pried wide open …

To unfurl a white carpet of snow…

The domain dreary, frigid, and inaccessible…

A Mazandaran brought back to life…

Koh-i-Maran, Koh-i-Sulaiman, Zabarwan and others…

Mirroring Alborz, Hara, and Damavand capped in snow…

Landscapes sheathed in a pristine veil…

As Bizhan and Manizeh in virginal embrace…

Denizens wrapped in layer after layer…

Rostam's Zereh, Joshan, and Babr-e-Bayan…

Consistent struggle for survival and success…

A Haft-Khan-e-Rostam for seventy days…

Days crawl like snails and nights stretch forever…

As Rakhsh, Shabdiz, and Shabrang tied to their harnesses…

Lords and servants alike scamper to warmer climes…

Like Sahrdaran, vaspuhran, wuzurgan, and azadan of yore…

Lock, stock, and barrel, the whole ensemble carried away…

An Akvan Div carrying fake Rostams of the day again…

Endless misery, apathy, and lack of redressal on time…

Inconsolable Tahmineh crying for dead Sohrab due to the lack of Noush daru…

Householders harassed by paucity of light, water, and earth…

As Kadag xwaday craving for the three feathers of the Simurgh…

Akvan Div, Arzhang Div, and Div-e-Sepid die too…

KayKavus is set free and the blood of Div-e-Sepid's heart cures him…

Blood of innocents marks the onset of spring…

"Khune Asyavushan" germinating the seeds of life…

Wouldn't a perennial winter bring glad tidings?

A Kashur Wande never to end…

HALF'S AND NONE'S

I miss the calluses of your hands massaging my neck…
The sound of my name rolling off your tongue…
I miss the warmth of life on your side of the bed…
The look in your eyes when you desired me…

I miss the hoarseness of your laughter echoing out…
The tears welling up in your eyes as you tried to stop…
I miss the odour of your body drenched in sweat …
The fragrant ittar dabbed behind your earlobes …

I miss holding you tight as we rode to the markets…
The sweet nothings that you'd try whispering to me…
I miss the intertwining of our fingers as we walked…
The pains you took to put a smile on my face…

I miss sitting near you as we sat to have our meals...
The secret kisses, winks, and sharing the servings…
I miss your impatient prancing, and furtive glances…
The restive behavior as I did my nightly chores…

I miss you lending me a hand in the farm we had…
The way you milked the cows and herded the sheep…
I miss wiping the sweat on your face with my dupatta…
The smile on your face as you sat down to have tea…

I miss the way you pampered my pregnancies, twice…
The jumping with joy as you held them in your hands…
I miss you fussing over every detail for the fairies…
The morning baths and the nighttime lullabies…

I miss you riding them to the school and madrassa…
The joy on your face when they mastered the basics…
I miss the manner you cuddled us all every time…
The fun we had in those outings in the days gone by…

They'd come out of nowhere and took you away for questioning...
Never to come back...

The rifle-butts to your back, the cracking of bones...
The kicks in your abdomen, your shrieks of pain...
The blood splattered all across, roses in blossom...
The helplessness in your eyes, the futile pleading...
The cries of the fairies, cowering in the corner...
The pain in my belly, the blurring of my vision...
The hands tied, being dragged away forever...
The bundling in the truck, gates of hell shut...

The billowing of dust in the wake...
or was it my life...

Solidarity from neighbours, help from friends...
Stains on the floor, stuck as obstinate reminders...
Frenetic visits to the camp, denials, and lies...
Visits by the fatigues, men in uniforms too...
Promises of enquiry, veiled threats in tow...
Cameras and flashlights, plus news highlights...
Politicians of all hues, repetitive empty rhetoric...
Activists and lobbyists, an impotent crop...

The pretensions and pain...
A futile exercise...

Visits to the morgues, near and distant...
Unknown cemeteries, exhumed bodies...
With buckled legs, trembling hands...
Wandering mind, an anxious heart...
Bodies in rows, frightening columns...
Wallets and watches, kids' photographs ...
Relief and respite, temporary in nature...
Hope renewed, an excuse for the fairies...

The charade of existence…

A big lie…

The seed within me, a part of you…

A subtle assurance, you continue to be…

The long days, cold, and lonely nights…

Nobody to hold me, no one to comfort…

The daily toil, an endless rigmarole…

Recurring nightmares, numbed soul…

The flashes of the past, like lost dreams…

Uncertain present, worries for future…

The ambivalence of life…

A bitter truth…

The pain and fatigue, a new life born…

She missed your Aadhaan, Iqamah too…

Somebody else stood up, earned sawaab…

No joy or laughter, tears wetting my cheeks…

A strange emptiness, blighting my soul…

Mind clouded, nerves frayed and defiant…

Taxed by obligations, bogged down by duties…

Every day a struggle, every night an ordeal…

The sanctimony of being…

A ritual of tolerance…

The preying eyes, the suggestive chatter…

The questions raised, the rumours spread…

The hollow haranguing, the willful harassment …

The constant cajoling, the subtle coercion…

The realities defined, the logic derailed…

The sympathy expressed, the empathy exhibited…

The Maulvis decree, four years are enough…

The faith unwavering, the will still resolute…

The complex societal paradox…

A challenge to free will…

A decade gone, countless blossoms seen but unfelt…

Flowering of precocious buds, and butterflies too…

Change of seasons, pages in a tattered book...

The blooming orchards, a withered heart…

Furrows on forehead, wrinkles under the eyes…

Some carved by uncertainty, others etched by yearning…

Grooming the fairies, persistent provocations…

The helplessness enduring, the evasive closure…

The orchestrations of time…

A journey unknown…

Elusive respite, effervescence of hope…

Winds of change, public consciousness…

Similar travails, worse tragedies too…

Bonds of pain built, voices in unison…

In freezing snow, relentless rain, and sleet…

Scorching heat , temperate breeze…

Marching in protests, manhandled often…

Hoarse cries, the voice lost on deaf ears…

The quest for justice…

A perennial struggle…

A symbolic gesture, a dubious intent…

Compensation hailed, a humane act…

Would it suffice, isn't it too little and too late…

Blood money it is, call it by any name…

Do you have a price tag, are you up for sale…
Can I sell your flesh, can I sell your blood..
What'll your soul fetch me, and your smile…
Or your memories, treasured in my heart…

The dignity of life…
A lopsided bargain…

Prospects bleak, misery in attendance…
But fairies passionate, primed for their future…
They share the mantle, contribute their mite…
Aches my heart, contrition my only solace…
Devils to vanquish, loadful of demons to slay…
To contend with life, challenge them every day…
Reluctant endeavour, to make up for your absence…
Not in a dream, did I wish this for myself…

The inevitability of future…
A prerogative of Nature…

Streaks of grey, the taut arteries across temples…
Speckles on my face, constant aches and pain…
Missing out on details, small or significant…
Mellowing down, cravings and dead desires…
Sleep long gone, dreams like lost friends…
All the trusses done, the constellations counted…
Bracing for vagaries, braving the vicissitudes…
Love has taken its toll, fidelity has paid a price…

The enigma of endurance…

A divine blessing…

The stigma persists, the questions remain…

The doubts embedded, the answers missing…

The apathy stifling, the indifference asphyxiating…

The pretence evident, the deception unnerving…

The truth buried deep, the lies galore in abundance…

The suffering unnoticed, the pain disregarded…

The loss crippling, the acknowledgement unheard…

The denouement awaited, the wait interminable…

I still stand there…

A placard in my hand…

They call me a Half – Widow…

But there are None's too…

AN ODE TO THE ALPHABETS OF KASHUR STOICISM

Do you feel abased because of your dreams?

Or is it your abhorrence for the allegory of your anguish?

Would abstention have helped assimilation or would it still mark you as an aberration?

Or is it an abstraction in abundance?

Long back you allowed yourself acclimatization with an accord…

Did that help you acclimatize or was that just an accomplice, acerbic and abrasive?

That which accentuated your abject state of being…

Or did you reckon that acquiescence shall ensure your acme?

Your adulation proved to be short-lived and there was nothing else to adorn with…

All that remained was acrimony, still adamant…

Soon admonishment followed and it was acute…

On its heels followed affinity and alacrity and that too withered into an advocacy of alienation…

With affliction and adversity in tow…

Affluence of thought, action, or state changed hands with aggrandizement of the agrarian ambit…

You were affable while you strove to preserve your aesthetic…

But altruism didn't ameliorate your agony…

Your allegiance lay elsewhere, called out the adroit…

And in your arteries gushed ambivalence and ambiguity…

I wonder, did you ever allude to an anachronism of freedom?

Or that the anomalies of antagonism would lead to anecdotes of annihilation…

What was witnessed had no antecedents or analogies to proffer?

Was this the reason for your apathy or was it an arbitrary act of antipathy?

You struggled to accept the antithetical archetype though the ardour assuaged all…

Ascetics and aristocrats attested the artifice of attribution…

Destiny allowed you an auspicious augury…

When the authoritarian was replaced by the austere authoritative…

Later the stars augmented avarice and the audacity was authentic…

Your avuncular ace attracted aversion…

Did it surprise you that even the alienation didn't affect atonement from that quarter?
Though assumptive and arcane were the artifacts of abnegation...
In sometime amnesty followed and acquittal too...
But the attire could neither avenge itself nor inspire awe...

Your narrative is nowadays dubbed as a banal ballad...
At every opportunity the bathetic brotherhood beckons bedlam...
And the barrage of barbarity has stripped your soul barren...
Doesn't it befuddle you to see the behemoth balked?
It's a baleful bane that beguiles from its bastion...
You've seen banter banished and brothers blooded...
Bullets baptize youth and belligerence brawl with benevolence...
Your betrothal with bellicosity is a bequest from your brow-beating benefactor...

Why do you feel beholden?
Is it because it behooves you to be benign?
Can't you even bemoan what has befallen you?
Aren't you bemused at your belittling that belies the bluster?
Here you are, besieged by bereavement...
But the buffoons are still bickering about your bifurcation...
Or shall we call it a bogus trifurcation?
Who will you beseech, or do they want you to beg?

Belittle, burden, besmirch; isn't that all that their brevity accomplishes?
Blasé is all you are now as you no longer blanch...
Even though bullets and blood are on a bohemian binge...
Blandishment and brazen breaches are bolstered by braggadocio...
Braggarts feigning bravado are bogus and bland...
Blasphemy is blatant and the bucolic has turned bleak...
Some thought that boycott and bandhs would turn out to be a boon...
But I believe that all that did was to bowdlerize the blithe and buoyant boyhood...

How can blunders so blatant ever bode well?
Especially when they've always brandished bias...
Brash and bellicose are the boys on the streets...
And bizarre is the banishment of boisterousness too...
You've been badgered to the brink...
A little more is probably all that you can bear...
Your body is bleeding and your soul torn bare...
Besieged and biased by the boorish boots...

The cacophony on the streets turned cadaverous...
As callow youth confronted capricious charlatans...
The calamity loomed large and turned out to be compelling...
The conundrum you are facing was contrived and chronic...
Complacent ghosts capitulated like a house of cards...
Chastisement was cultivated as a smug collateral...
To your chagrin, civility was dealt a coup-de-grâce...
And circumlocution confirmed as a political compulsion...

Conciliatory overtures and talk of clemency took centre-stage...
But wasn't the cause lost by delayed consensus and conflation?
Chords of blood, parents, siblings and all sought catharsis ...
Even that was denied as contrition ceased to exist...
The collusion in culpability is civil in countenance...
And corroborated by a conspicuous absence of conformity...
Commerce is cumbersome as the conflagration is averse to its continuity...
Your losses are colossal and the compensation, a caricature of commensuration...

For centuries you promoted a confluence of cultures...
And witnessed a concord of communities....
But they contaminated its credence as a confabulation...
Convivial conversations were chided as being controversial...

Millennia of cordiality and camaraderie were ceded to cynicism…
Covert and clandestine were their consistent conclaves…
The contamination was copious and cogent in nature…
They made them cower and appear craven and crestfallen…

They castigated your charisma as chimerical…
And your commodious heart as contrived with conceit…
Their cynicism curtailed their credibility and powers of circumspection…
This consolidation culminated in chaos and consternation…
You were not commiserated or offered any consolation…
The condemnation was consummate and conspicuous by its cynicism…
Curiously you still cajole and cultivate the conservation of your essence…
But doesn't the cursorily composed narrative appear confounding?

Fathers and mothers, sisters and brothers…
Husbands and wives, sons and daughters…
Didn't you exhort them to call out death, disappearance, and disability?
Request them to dally and dawdle with time and probability…
The defiance had swept across your demographics…
But surprisingly they dubbed its genesis as diabolical…
Soon the deluge became a rallying point of dissonance…
Still unsure whether that debunked or deluded the Two-Nation theory…

Though disenfranchised and disgruntled are your denizens…
You never faced any dearth of dauntless devils…
Their dexterity was debilitating and deleterious…
Their demeanour proved to be detrimental to their disposition …
But soon duplicity and deception took over…
You stood decimated and defamed by your dilettantes…
I understand that you tried to dissimulate your dejection…
It took you a while to understand that the die had been cast for the debacle…

You dared your deviant descendants to denounce the dissonance...
And that desolation and depravity shall be the fruits of their deeds...
But your patience was depleted and discord ran amuck...
Didactic diatribes didn't deter the dichotomy of destiny ...
Diffidence and discrepancies made you disconcerted...
The devout became disingenuous and discreet, a deadly damnation...
Disjointed and dismal were pronounced as your hallmarks...
Your edifice was dismantled and destitution coupled with despair...

Folks dealt with dystopian drudgery and dogmatic dissuasion...
Thankfully, the dormant durability came to the fore with disdain ...
All those docile and dreary lives dissipated their disheveled and disfigured demeanours...
And turned a dispassionate ear to the disparaging distortions...
The overtures deemed as dubious and dissolute...
You decried the denigration and the degradation dispensed to you...
They dwelled in dominance and denunciation as an add-on...
Truth disseminated as a disposable distillation of distraction...

You evoked the ebullience of love and eclectic persuasions...
Alongwith the effervescence and effulgence of innocence...
Your bosom germinated seeds of an egalitarian efflorescence...
And epitomized the endearing ensemble of your all-embracing credo...
But weren't you forewarned about the egregious and egotistical political elements?
The ones who enticed to encumber and eschew your emancipation...
Their embellished endeavours, an exercise in erratic ennui...
Enticement did extort some but is still largely elusive...

There were epochs of epiphany and euphoria...
Your exposition was one of eloquent elucidation...
But that was exploited by internecine extirpation and endemic execration...
The exotic era relegated as an evanescent entity...

They know that your enigma is eternal and your ethos ethereal...
But then what makes them excoriate your efforts and why?
Aren't you an euphemism for what they were in the past?
Why haven't they evolved and why don't they exhibit equanimity?

Is prejudice embryonic and exploitation a de rigueur for nation states?
Is human empathy empirical or an equivocal expectation?
We'd callously witnessed an exodus before and sometime back that of an entire creed...
Why did we disengage and not shine as beacons of hope again?
Was it the lure of enchantment or the fear of extermination?
You had examples of excoriation for the evil done but were they enough?
An entire ethnicity expunged and the perpetrators exculpated?
The expiation was expedited by the extermination of the entrapped...

Extrapolations and expectations aside, the empathy of creeds stays eternal...
The exuberance of engagements still exudes effusively...
Friends of yore still extoll their experiences and exult about memories...
And neighbours who lived next door enthrall each other with esoteric encounters...
Thankfully, the exquisite bonds are extant in eternity...
But you incurred an exorbitant expenditure in suffering and prejudice...
For you, obviously the inclusivity has been expatiated as being existential...
Erudition and enterprise, beauty and humility are extrinsically intertwined...

Falsehoods continue to be fabricated forging fresh facets for inference...
You may consider it facetious but the execution is facile...
Divided into factions which subscribe to these fallacies...
Such forays in fallibility have forced your youth to fallow...
To see the honchos falter is a familiar sight for you since ages...
Since long have you faced a famine of fastidious faces...
All you've reaped is a fatuous crop feeding failure...
It's farcical for the others but has proved fatal for you...

Others find it feasible to fawn for your fealty...
Your fickle ones feign it fervently and garner felicity...
But there's something that these feckless fools don't understand...
A fiasco is a fiasco by any other name too...
The immoral display finesse in filibustering...
Don't they know that you are finicky and your forbearance is finite?
Their firebrands are flabbergasted at the fissures...
Flailing at your firmament in a flagrant fashion...

You've tried telling them that flippancy shall make them flounder...
That fluke of accession is not a fortuitous recipe for flourishing...
You've been in a constant flux and their faux pas have flustered them...
When shall they admit that the foibles of a few can fizzle out the future of the masses?
Others persist in fomenting trouble though some attempt to forestall...
How long shall your life blood serve as elixir for those famished for blood?
You were warned by a foreboding but nobody could foresee the forces of evil all around...
Foreshadows and forecasts all failed to forge a focussed approach...

Forlorn fathers, distraught mothers, helpless wives, and half widows...
Fragile sisters, frail brothers, anxious friends, and nervous neighbours...
Peace and prosperity forfeited by fraud fostered by furtive fiends...
Is that the forte of the formidable forces aligned against you?
How can friendships be forged by fragile and fractured faith?
And frugal generosity fortified by fulminating forums...
Frenetic frenzy has stripped them of their fulsome façade...
Has your fragrant fortress been willed into the final frontier?

You had the gall to galvanize the gallant...
The gamut of emotions was germinal in the least...
From the genuine gentry to the landed gentility...
And the garrulous sweat shops and fields flush with crops...

Generations have genuflected in a germane garb at your unshackling altar...
Genial and genteel, the gaunt and the gaudy, across gender and genre...
They blamed your genes but you knew that they meant it to be generic...
Your genealogy has been corrupted and garbled with generalizations...

What they gestated you with has germinated now...
Whether it's ghastly or genteel, the gerrymandering won't do now...
They would gloat with glee and glower to goad...
For death is a gourmand now and gluttonous in appetite...
In these glum times, you gauge a glimmer of hope...
Irrespective of the glib and giddy talk that garnishes their guile...
You've gleaned the gist of great things to come...
In the glut of globalization, your groans and grievances are being heard loud...

You have graduated from the gossamer to all things gory...
And your blood and flesh from gullible and guileless to vile and crafty...
They are constantly grappling to gratify and grease their own palms...
The gratitude they all owe you has been deemed gratuitous...
It saddens you to have your grandeur gorged upon gruffly...
You were a grand entity before they even came to the fore...
Yet they are smug with their grandiloquent vision of justice and equality...
Though they persevere with their denial of your nationhood...

Gnarled they appear with a grimace on their guise in this game...
Grandiose is the pedestal that they view and govern you from...
They grudge you your gumption and grace in this grueling ordeal...
Though none of them entertains gripes about their grievous acts...
Groggy and groveling in fear is what they all have left your folks...
Those genial and gregarious souls, good natured and gingerly in demeanour...
Gone are those times when you were guided by deceptive Arthurs and treacherous knights...
Now you've girded every man and woman as your knight and dame...

In halcyon days, you were a habitat of the hale and hearty…
Hallowed was the realm as the land of harmony…
Heathens and the faithful, haggard and the haughty…
All dwelled as habitués of this blessed haven…
No one was harried and nobody harangued…
From those with hauteur to those deemed hapless…
The headstrong and the haughty haggled to hasten havoc…
Everybody failed to decipher the harbingers of harrowing turmoil…

The much hackneyed hallmark of beauty and hope that you always have been…
Was haphazardly hyped as a product of habitual hearsay…
The hegemon heedlessly committed a heinous crime to safeguard his heritage…
A new hegemony replaced the previous one with the heir still in reckoning…
Nonetheless you had hoped that this would herald a brighter tomorrow…
Unfortunately, that was and still is akin to a Herculean labour…
Your bosom heaved with pain as they hewed and hacked you…
Sacrilege and heresy followed as civility was pushed into hibernation…

The hermitage of heterogeneity has long been paid its last homage…
The hirelings have honed their histrionics to aid their heterodoxy…
Sadly, the hiatus brought back the hierarchies of hermetic pretensions…
But you know that your history is replete with flags changing colours…
Hostile and horrendous, the horde unleashed a new league of horrors…
Still they haven't been able to harm your honour and halt your hospitality
Across the horizon masters pulling their strings are hortatory by habit…
And their hubris prods them on for your humiliation…

Their homilies are suffused with humanitarian hoaxes…
Fuelled by hyperbole, characterized by hype, and hypocritical in nature…
They've used heuristics to fuel hysteria across every hearth and hovel…
The hieroglyphics of their intentions yet to be deciphered…

To heckle and hinder has been a hybrid of their hilarious strategies...
They hurt and haemorrhaged the heroes that you hinged your hopes on...
Time and again they've have hoarded your skulls and souls...
The Jews have had theirs, wasn't it time for your own Holocaust...

You've borne a few iconoclasts and bred idealists ...
Impressive ideologues and intimidating demagogues too...
Some harped on their ideologies and others exhibited their idiosyncrasies...
Across your idyllic locales and inspiring vistas...
Your illustrious sons and daughters have done you proud...
And yes, there has been no dearth of ignominious ones along the way...
Some imbibed the lessons of history from times immemorial...
While others impaired your legacy to script their own immortality...

The current imbroglio was imperceptible but impending nevertheless...
The powers that be stayed imperious and imprudent as ever...
Impregnable were their bastions before they capitulated to impetuous tides...
The implosion was impromptu as implicit was their doom...
The inception of a milieu triggered an incitement of the masses...
Some implored for sanity as the resistance was inchoate and incipient too...
But the parvenus inaugurated hell with impunity...
Knowing little that they were inane incarnations of incendiary evil...

Incorrigibly immoral and incompetent were the incumbents...
Soon they became inconspicuous and indifferent to the ethos...
Insolence and iniquity became the operating trademark of the new spawn...
Incredulous were their deeds and indelible was their writ...
The impecunious and the indigent swelled their ranks and so did the opportunists...
You noticed that morality and history ceased to be an impediment in their inflammatory acts...
Sadly, you could not indenture your inalienable right to your cultural continuity...
They attained infamy by infringing and trampling it insidiously...

History is a witness to your indomitable spirit…
The indignation imposed is inexorable, though some treated it as inevitable…
Even if it was innocuous or infinitesimal, or an insolent innuendo…
You've always been insuperable and never succumbed to ingratiation
Though they've been innately insidious and insatiable yet not inscrutable…
Intransigence and intimidation earned them irrelevance and irreverence...
Your introspection of the insurrection is interjected with intrepid episodes...
But you are aware that it's intrinsic, ineffable, intangible, and interminable…

Come winter and you witness the jading of the jollity…
The jingoists halt their junkets and jettison their fiery jargon…
Unpredictably, the juggernaut jejunes into a jeery jaunt…
Those who jeopardized peace and livelihood jostle for justifications…
But you observe the jubilation of some at this juncture…
And those too who are jovial in demeanour and judicious by pretense…
The juxtaposition of the juveniles with the junta is jocular in the least…
The jurisprudence gets jolted into action in its jittery jurisdiction…

The keffiyah clad kernels have jousted with the kingsmen…
A kidnapping and some kickoffs kissed the Khedive's kilt…
You are the modern day Kohinoor they deign as kosher for them…
Killing and maiming kindness and humanity along the way…
They all want you as a jewel in their crowns…
They've juggled and jived to snatch you as a jackpot…
But they feel jilted, jealous, and jinxed in this Minotauran jigsaw…
So these jackals slit your jugulars with jagged bayonets…

From kids to kindred souls, across knolls and knots…
All those who kneaded and kindled this spirit in kinship…
They languish and languor to witness a legitimate solution…
You witness some lampoon and others lament their losses…

The liaison between ire and anger has long been latent…
But don't you know that liabilities can never legitimize lassitude…
Levity and legerdemain cannot assure you a legacy…
Lethargy can prove lethal on your road to legitimacy…

You have had to seek leverage against a leviathan…
Though your efforts have been laughed off as Lilliputian …
Nothing has been spared to liquidate your lineage…
But in the process they ended up lionizing you…
Ludicrous litigation has become lucrative for your Lucifers…
The folks are lugubrious and the future worried about its longevity…
In the lull lie the lurking leeches to steal your dreams and happiness…
Little do they know that your limpid lustre shall forever stay luminous…

You've been maculated with machinations since antiquity…
Ranging from the macabre to the malevolent in nature…
Unethical and fickle politicians swamped you with maladies…
From a malice for morality to a malaise of fickleness…
Undeterred by the magnitude of these maelstroms…
Where malevolence tried to dampen your magnanimity…
Or malapropisms of deceit tried to maim your magnificence…
Nature colluded with your stoicism to eternalize your majestic disposition…

Even those who claimed themselves as the manifestation of your aspirations…
Turned out to be malignant as they proved to be malingerers of morality…
The innocent masses, malleable and prone to manipulation…
Always end up as martyrs on one altar or the other…
In this matrix of loss, suffering, pain, and melancholia…
They've meandered from mayhem to mediation…
As maudlin and mawkish mavens have mauled and marred their existence…
They've matured and metamorphosed into mutinous mavericks …

Some sons of soil, who mendaciously dub themselves as mendicants of liberation,
Menacing and melodramatic at best, proved nothing but an impotent menagerie...
Brothers-in-arms across the wall, meager in impact and manifold in number...
Cohorts from within and mercenaries at large, methodical and meticulous...
From marauding militants to meretricious minions in tow...
Motley morons and misanthropes to incorrigible miscreants...
They all tried their worst to brand you as a metaphor for mercantile exploitation...
Thankfully, you, as always, proved that their misconstruction was just a myth...

In this melee of misfortunes and misjudgments...
You almost became a mnemonic for monotonous, miserable memorabilia...
A microcosm of humanity in action, though a miniscule minority...
You've maintained your mores and mitigated the miseries ...
Right from your mythical chants to the monotheistic creed...
Across milieus and millennia, golden epochs or dark eras...
Across mutinies and migrations, events mundane and momentous...
You've mesmerized multitudes and mollified all with your munificence...

Soon after their apocryphal zenith, the homebreds touched their nadir...
Their narrative nullified and presence negated as a nuisance...
The naïve folks navigated the nefarious designs of the necromancers...
While the pseudo-nationalists took centre stage to negate their own nuances...
The persuasions of synapses against this rigmarole are nascent and nebulous entities...
Years of negativity and neglect have soured the nectar of belief and trust...
The Kashur intellect is yet to succumb to the neologisms of the turncoats' lexicon...
You proved to be their nemesis while they tried to negotiate it as a necessity...

Right-wing, left-wing, centrists, ideological narcissists and apparatchiks...
Southside political nihilists, all created networks to neutralize your spirit...
The neutral neophytes wriggled and niggled to occupy a niche...
The nauseating ones soon realized the futility of navigation...

But in their neurotic naiveté, they forged a nexus of evil and abomination…
And in doing so brought to naught their pretensions of nobleness…
The new nomenclature of your defiance nibbled at their edifice …
The global embarrassment and censure nullified their credentials of a just society…

The novelty of untruths represents the regression of purpose, thought, and action…
Yet it has only served to nourish their notoriety…
Notable is the absence of a will to nurture goodwill…
So every noble endeavour gets relegated to the backburner of history…
While nubility is ravished and young lives nullified…
Honour is made negotiable and survival necessitated as a priority…
Dissent is cloaked as sedition that renders every law as nugatory…
New-age numismatists collect corpses and futures…

You are nostalgic about those days gone by…
An era of peace and prosperity with violence null and void…
Nowadays nervousness has ousted nonchallance …
And uncertainty has badgered nonconformity into submission…
The sanctity of life is a non-entity in the parlance of neutralization…
With liberty, dignity, and freedom of choice a noetic hallucination…
The notion of your normative existence has become a non-descript nomad…
Your nightmares are no longer nocturnal but witnessed in broad daylight now…

Even your worst detractors consider you an oasis of syncretic synergy…
Where the obdurate and the obedient in faith pay their obeisance…
Though their objectives included obfuscating the tolerant ethos…
Being oblivious to the strength of your credo, they now face obloquy…
You had been obligated since ages to be politically correct…
And the ones leading that bandwagon have been the obsequious spawn…
Their obstinacy trolled you with that redundant and obscure logic of unity in diversity…
But time and again you've hollered them down with your obstreperousness…

Their pawns irritatingly obtrusive and shockingly obtuse...
And their odious clangs that occupy you heaped with public odium...
They've placed their faith in an occult of obviation and obliteration...
And strive to occlude the odoriferous wafts of your will and choice...
Your odyssey of loss, pain, and suffering was scripted by the odious oligarchy of evil...
Offensive and ominous has been their onslaught on your being...
Omnipotent, omnipresent, omniscient has been their projected personification...
It's a different story that even this opiate has not saved them their opprobrium...

You've faced them in the past and you are still facing all kinds of oppressors...
What unites them is opportunism and their efforts to offset each other...
Oracles on one side of the fence talk about omens and opportunities for your future...
And orators on the other side wax lyrical about opportune timings of resistance or reprisals...
The obnoxious twins oppress by fear, intimidation, and ordinances of morbid origins...
Weeding out opposition, faking outreach, and ostracizing dissent...
Through all this, your folks continue to bear the onerous onus of their sanity...
Their optimism has scripted an epic opus of endurance and survival...

The ostensibly orthodox oscillate between conscience and conflation...
Yet your outrage at their ostentatious lifestyles fizzles out as an otiose memory...
While others commit outrageous atrocities across cities, towns, and the outskirts...
Overweening and overbearing are those officious offenders...
Though overwhelming in number and overzealous in their responses ...
Somehow you've managed to outwit their overt as well as covert machinations...
However, even though you are overwrought and overcome with exhaustion ...
One day, Insha'Allah, you shall overthrow the oxymoron of malicious benevolence...

In this pandemonium which is perennially pervasive across your realms...
Partisans and patriots alike have proffered you exits from the quagmire...
Plebiscite, referendum, independence, merger, autonomy, or status-quo populate their panacea...
You see some options being palliative at best though some may turn out to be paradoxical too...

Pacifism and peace are parodied as paradigms of weakness by one and all…
Patronizing attitudes and one-upmanship has perpetuated your unbridled passion…
The pedagogy of political exhortations is pedantic at best…
Strangely, there is no paucity of perfidious personalities though penitents are rare…

Survival and sustenance is a perilous exercise for the plebeians and patricians alike…
You are now a personification of patience and persistence…
It appears as if a perpetuation of pernicious pain is aiming for its pinnacle…
A plethora of repetitive propositions is supposed to placate your pathos…
The portents are plausible and poignantly pertinent...
Nevertheless, there is no pause in your plunder and pillage…
But you are comforted by the assurance that the pompous shall perish…
And your plight shall become pliable and your demeanour implacable…

The pretenders and potentates who occupy your sacred throne…
Have no regard for the Preamble or their obligations to posterity…
Their misplaced pragmatism has set up a host of precarious precedents…
Those serve as a premonition of privation and provocation for times to come…
You know that their predominance and preponderance has misled them…
And misguided them into believing it to be their prerogative to prevaricate…
While others adopting primitive cultures have tried to pollute your pristine being…
Smug in their precocious intellect that warrants them perpetuity of power…

Pusillanimous as well as pugnacious are your folks on the streets…
Puerile protégés and profligate prodigals counter them from positions of power…
Every stakeholder has displayed a propensity to prognosticate…
Some are prone to pontification while others attempt to propel themselves into prominence…
You are shocked by the lack of propriety of the puissant…
Though they unabashedly pronounce their prowess in breaking promises…
There is talk about a potent and propitious prophecy…
That the return to your proverbial peace and prosperity is preordained…

You are fabled as a quaint version of heaven on earth…
A haven of quietude and quintessence of simplicity and harmony you were…
But decades have been squandered in quibbles and quarrels over your overlordship…
A quirk of fate has turned you into a quagmire of death and deprivation…
Quarantines are set up without any qualms and everyone quivers about getting quashed…
Quorums of expression and quantums of protest get dubbed as querulous…
From your quarries, youth and modesty are mined to quell the questions…
You wonder when the queues shall end and the blood-thirst get quenched…

Raconteurs regale your generations with anecdotes past and present…
About repression and restraint, radicalization, and rancour…
The rapes of innocence and ravishing of entire communities…
Of rambunctious Rambos ravaging womanhood of its dignity…
Unfortunately, the ravenous homebreds didn't occupy any rarefied niche too…
Ruthless to the core, they were no less repugnant and soiled and sawed numerous souls…
Cries for justice met with rampant rationalizations adding salt to your wounds…
And many more were stifled for the fear of reprisals from snakes in your own hearth…

This and more has had its ramifications across the realm …
Hurt and rebellious, or radical and recalcitrant, all recoiled at the horrors…
You've witnessed the recants and rebuttals of the old ways of life…
Reconciliation is passé and the refutation of the regime is in…
Though recrimination hasn't helped either nor has remediation on any front…
But the rectitude of the masses has prevailed to rejuvenate you…
You emerged as redoubtable but they called it regression…
Tell me, don't you relish your recondite relevance?

Without any recompense and refurbishment they talk about redressal…
While in reality they've all but relinquished their responsibility…
Doesn't that appear to be reminiscent of a bygone era to you?
When imperialism tried to stifle and relegate humanity to the backburner…

Remorseless and relentless is your march towards your destiny…
While they renege on their commitments and threaten you with repercussions…
The blood of the innocents has replenished your resolve…
Though they continue to repudiate and repress in a reprehensible manner…

Your masses are restive and the valleys resonant with resurgence…
The inhuman reprisals have compounded the revulsion…
Retribution is in the air and renunciation in every heart and soul…
Those revered for their rhetoric have been reviled in a relapse…
Rudderless and renegade is how they describe the hapless men and women…
What other recourse can the repressed resort to if retribution is what they offer?
What they don't understand is that restitution alone can't resuscitate them?
The time of reckoning is approaching fast as you stay resolute and refulgent…

Travellers, monarchs, scions, and seers waxed eloquent about your salubrious climes…
The solitude you offer, the synthesis of cultures, and the sanctity of existence celebrated…
They'd be rolling in their graves nowadays to see you struggling for survival…
What with unscrupulous entities slashing and scrounging you in their sordid attempts?
The common man has stayed sagacious and sanguine throughout the strife…
But nothing is sacrosanct now and every day you witness a sacrilege of humanity…
Your suffocated gasps for emancipation and smothered cries for justice are dubbed as seditious...
And your efforts to reclaim your identity tagged as secessionary…

A Divine satire is being staged for all those filled with hate and scorn…
But does truth ever count and logic appeal to those satiated with speculation…
Their sophists with their specious chatter always attempt to drive schisms in your brood…
They are scathing, even sardonic in their criticism and seek to slander and scare…
Their stance has stagnated for decades now and their overtures exposed as spurious
But seamless and sedulous are your sentiments and sibylline your exhortations…
They squandered every opportunity and stifled every voice to suit their agenda…
Yet you thank the heavens for not having your legacy ridiculed as serendipitous…

You have nothing against those summoned from down south...
Some are there for subsistence and sustenance and some to shape their futures...
Your superannuating sycophants witness regimes supplanting and superseding each other...
Like similes of shame, they continue to seek their sumptuous bacchanalia and sybaritic jaunts...
Satanic and supercilious in demeanour and surreptitious in their scheming...
They are overzealous in their superimpositions and supererogatory in their suppressions...
You are shocked to admit that you bore them in your womb and suckled them with your breasts...
Yet they do not shy away from spilling your blood and shaming your pride...

Your pain is not superficial but subliminal and your loss stultifying...
But you've chosen not to be a sedentary spectator who finds solace in subjugation...
Whether subversive or subservient, their deeds have sequestered them and scared your folks...
But they've failed to sully your soul and subdue your spirit...
Spontaneous or sporadic, they are unable to interpret the succinct and seminal struggle...
Their attempts at your subordination have challenged your steadfastness in vain...
You still retain your sentient sobriety and your solitude to fall back upon...
And mock their stubbornness that doesn't even let them squiggle out of this stalemate...

What do you think is your talisman against tyranny and terror?
Is it your temporal tenacity or your belief in the tenets of your faith?
You often wonder what has taxed you more...
The trials subjected by one or the tribulations imposed by the other...
They colluded to torture and taint your flesh and soul...
But you proved to be tougher than what they'd thought and trained for...
To some these reflections are nothing but a tautological tirade...
But to you they tantamount to a tariff levied by time...

Trespassers across the ages have displayed the temerity to taunt your consciousness...
You triumphed over emperors fair and square but fell to treachery time and again...
Some targeted you for territory and treasures and some to set up theocracies...
Tenuous and tangential have been these tenures but on every occasion you've stood tall...

They made your folks toil in treacherous terrain' n' climes and claimed their skulls as trophies...
Some drowned them as bagfuls in the tranquil Dal while others burned them alive in dung...
Many were tried for their faith and many more hanged without trial for fictional treason...
Their travails made them truculent and helped you terminate these transitions in history...

Your folks thrived under the tutelage of your history, culture, and faith...
Little did they foresee the travesties of nature yet to transpire...
The tranquility of the realm gave way to tumult and trepidation...
As your folks started to tread tremulously on a torrid trip...
What was hoped for by suppliants as transitory got entrenched in time and space...
As the shutdowns increased torpidity and imposed torpor...
You dismissed as trifling, the tantalizing possibilities touted by the totalitarian setup...
Your folks are trenchant and immune to the transgressions of decadence and corruption...

What you've borne so far appears to be transcendental in nature...
The angels of history have been transfixed in attention to your turmoil...
You are on the threshold of a glorious historical epoch...
Someday tomes shall be written celebrating your tenaciousness...
The journey till date has been dangerously tedious and traumatic but telling too...
And your temperament has successfully withered the vagaries of time...
Someday folks shall throng to hear about your throes of pain and suffering...
And to hail your heroism and traduce the turpitude of the oppressors...

The fatigues are ubiquitous and the motives ulterior...
Their prejudice is unalterable and your stance unambiguous...
You took umbrage over the unabashed ultimatums...
As your unassuming folks are undaunted in their resolve to stand up against terror...
The honchos as usual are unapproachable and the miseries of the common man unappreciated...
Unbridled are the masses though and their fervour unassailable...
Nothing looks unattainable to you now and unconditional are their demands...
Unconventional is your response nowadays and unanimous is the approach...

The barbarity of their reprisals is unconscionable and your pain unmitigated ...
Unjustified are their acts and unlicensed are these uncouth and unkempt jackals of war...
Uncanny is the resemblance to those uncharted days of yore...
When your youth was unencumbered and unfettered...
Whatever they seek is unexceptionable though others find that unacceptable...
You are unequivocal in your understanding and yet they undermine that every time...
The mass participation underscores your standing and unity across the board...
But renders their justifications unfounded and the shock unfathomable...

The unctuous politicians are unparalleled in their guile and deception...
Unprincipled by nature, unsavoury in their morality, they tried to applying unguents...
But their intentions were unraveled in no time, none of them unpretentious...
Unprepossessing at the onset, they soon regressed to entertain their power lust...
Unsightly and unseemly have been their actions so far...
But unrelenting has been your opposition and uninhibited your strides...
The purity of your aspirations has been unimpeachable and universal their condemnation...
You've had to resort to unorthodox ways but unprecedented has been their brutality too...

Your resistance been unremitting and unrelenting since the onset of the Dark Ages...
Though unfortunately, you are not unscathed or unsullied at all...
Untoward and unwarranted are the subtexts of their crimes against you...
That's exactly the reason for their untenability and unacceptability...
From the youth on the streets to the urbane set in their castles...
Unwavering and unyielding are the hallmarks of your existence...
Even though they usurp dreams and engage in the usury of life and death...
But you shall have your utopia one day...

Vacuous and vainglorious are the worshippers of lead and brass...
Vain and vile are these inhuman visages of callousness and cruelty...
You have braved the vagaries and vicissitudes of history with aplomb...
Even when life became a variable and honor a vassal of violence...

The coffins of your valiant folks are a testimony of their valor...
The sacrifices of your venerable fallen shall not go in vain...
In the verdant valleys and across the vanguards of vanity ...
Who is the victor and who is being vanquished?

Across your vast reaches and the vantage of their strongholds...
Shrouded by the veneer of vehemence and vapid significance...
The vendors of vendetta choose their venues of validation...
The vaunted and the venal vie for dominance and veracity...
The verisimilitude of their pronouncements waxes and wanes with their viciousness...
Their versatility and venturesomeness is a reflection of their villainy...
You are vexed by the verbosity and the verbiage of their enunciations...
Isn't verity the simplest form of verification?

The vignettes sketched by history talk about vagrants of all ages...
Some vacillated between extermination and expulsion others had to vacate...
The current crop is vindictive and violent and they persist in your villification...
Virulent and vicious without precedent, they spew venom and vitriol...
However, the verve of your vernal harvest is a sign of your strength...
Vigorous and vibrant, vigilant and valorous is your pride...
Their virtues stand vindicated and values reinforced by time...
As their aspirations are valid and dreams voluminous in scale...

You credo has been the veneration of disparate beliefs...
Though the vice in the vicinity has been vituperative in its onslaught...
The viability of your cultural credentials was never in question...
But your vitality was gnawed at and temporarily rendered vulnerable ...
The volatility of the decades and the voracious evil did create a void ...
But your virtuosity in your vocation of human dignity fuelled your vitals...
You wonder when you shall reclaim your virginal vistas...
And forever put to rest the vanities of your destiny...

The muffled wails of the widows waft endlessly through the air…
Of fathers and mothers too trying coming to terms with their wanton loss…
Brothers and sisters trying to wangle and warble in make belief worlds…
Their faces winced with pain and somber visages wistful in the least…
Waifs with wasted childhoods and wary appurtenances of reality…
Wicked accoutrements of their efflorescence robbing them of their rights…
Wan and weary are the hearts of your folks and their souls wallow in pain…
But their will is resolute to wrestle and wrest what is rightfully theirs…

From their warrens they step out to wade in your blood…
They waylay your happiness and wean away your prosperity…
Then there are the wayward too trying to wend your course…
Your miseries wax and wane in their consonance and whims…
They crack their whips to make you writhe in pain…
And wreak their wrath to wither and whittle you down…
But what they haven't realized in their willful wiles is
That you are wrought in faith and forged in conviction…

Day in and day out you withstand the winnowing of loss and pain…
And you wrangle and wheedle with death to save some souls in debt…
But witless and whimsical is the wanderlust of suffering…
Wistfully you wish for a waiver from the wrench it wields…
Wicked and wretched is the welter of their wizened wizards…
It is their wont to wring you of your conscience and commitment…
But to you the whiff of liberty is like a wondrous windfall …
You've sacrificed your welfare to warrant that watershed in time…

You yearn to throw away the yoke of slavery and servitude…
And safeguard the sanctity and the identity of your culture…
Like a winsome wraith you dream of the days of yore…
For the yeomen of your dreams they appear to be yonder…
Even Zino of Citium won't dare to question your stoicism…
Zealous are your folks to feel the zephyr of unshacklement…
Zero or zilch is not what your future portends for you…
Haven't you been promised a zenith for all times to come…

The Kashur is still strong…

The Kashur is still defiant…

The Kashur is still proud…

The Kashur is still resolute…

The Kashur is still patient…

The Kashur is still resilient…

The Kashur is still affable…

The Kashur is still alive…

The Kashur still stands tall…

GLOSSARY

Aatish: Persian word for fire or ambers.

Abhinavagupta: Abhinavagupta [Circa 950–1016 C.E.] was a philosopher, mystic, and aesthetician from Kashmir. His largest and most famous work is *Tantrāloka,* an encyclopedic treatise on all the philosophical and practical aspects of Trika and Kaula [known today as Kashmiri Shaivism].

Abu Simbel: The Abu Simbel temples are two massive rock temples at Abu Simbel in southern Egypt. The twin temples, a UNESCO World Heritage Site, were originally carved out of the mountainside during the reign of Pharaoh Ramesses II in the 13th century BC, as a lasting monument to himself and his queen Nefertari, to commemorate his victory at the Battle of Kadesh.

Accession: The Instrument of Accession was the legal document designed to bring about accession. It was executed by the Government of India on the one hand and by the rulers of each of the princely states, individually, on the other. Amongst the more notorious of such accessions was the one executed by Maharaja Hari Singh, ruler of the State of Jammu and Kashmir, on 26 October 1947 by ignoring the popular sentiment.

ACK Comics: Amar Chitra Katha comics usually figuring historical or mythological characters of India or Hinduism.

Afrasiab: According to the *Shahnameh,* Afrasiab is the king and hero of Turan and an arch-enemy of Iran. In Iranian mythology, Afrasiab is considered by far the most prominent of all Turanian kings; he is a formidable warrior, a skilful general, and an agent of Ahriman, who is endowed with magical powers of deception to destroy Iranian civilization.

AFSPA: The draconian Armed Forces [Special Powers] Act [AFSPA], is an act of the Parliament of India that grants special powers to the Indian Armed Forces in what the Act terms as "disturbed areas". An act passed in 1990 was applied to Jammu and Kashmir and has been in force since then. The Act has received criticism from several sections for alleged concerns about human rights violations in the regions of its enforcement. When India presented its second periodic report to the United Nations Human Rights Committee in 1991, members of the UNHRC asked numerous questions about the validity of the AFSPA. They questioned the constitutionality of the AFSPA under Indian law and asked as to how it could be justified in light of the Article 4 of the International Covenant on Civil and Political Rights, ICCPR. On 23rd March 2009, UN Commissioner for Human Rights, Navanethem Pillay asked India to repeal the AFSPA. HRW have condemned human rights abuses in Kashmir by armed forces such as "extra-judicial executions", "disappearances", and torture under the aegis of the "Armed Forces Special Powers Act", which "provides impunity for human rights abuses and fuels cycles of violence.

Aharbal: Aharbal is known for its waterfall, Aharbal Falls, where the Veshu falls noisily 25 meters by 7 meters through a narrow gorge of granite boulders. Aharbal Falls are also referred to as the Niagara Falls of Kashmir, owing to the volume of the water that falls. Aharbal is a base for adventure tourism. The Veshu River is stocked with trout.

Ahriman: Angra Mainyu is the Avestan-language name of Zoroastrianism's hypostasis of the "destructive spirit". The Middle Persian equivalent is Ahriman.

AK: Russian [Avtomat Kalashnikova] A Kalashnikov automatic rifle series used by the militants and Indian armed forces in Kashmir.

Akvan Div: In Ferdowsi's Shahnameh, *Akvan* is described as having long hair, blue eyes, and a head like an elephants with a mouthful of tusks instead of teeth. In one of the tales, the demon traps Rostam while the hero is asleep, and carries him up into the sky and throws him in the sea. Rescuing himself from the waters, Rostam recovers his horse and confronts the demon again, subsequently beheading it.

Alborz: In Shahnameh, the mountain in Ērānvēj is named *Alborz* and considered sacred by Iranians.

Ama Baedaene Kulfi: Ama Baede [literally Old Ama] The Kulfi [local Ice cream] prepared by this renowned Kulfi maker in downtown Srinagar.

Amir-i- Kabir: Mir Syed Ali bin Shahab-ud-Din Hamadani [1314–1384] was a Persian Sūfī of the Kubrāwī order, a poet, and a prominent Shafi'i Muslim scholar. He was born in Hamadan, died in Kunar, and was buried in Khatlan. He played a major role in spreading Islam in Kashmir and he has also influenced the culture of the Kashmir valley. He was known as "Shāh Hamadhān" ["King of Hamadhān", Iran] and as *Amīr-i Kabīr* ([The Great Commander]. He wrote several short works on spirituality and Sufism. He has influenced the works of his contemporary in Kashmir, the female Śaiva poet Lallēśvārī.

Anglo-Sikh Wars: The Anglo-Sikh wars were a series of 1840s conflicts between the British East India Trading Company and the Sikh Empire and were as follows: The First Anglo-Sikh War [1845–46 C.E.] and The Second Anglo-Sikh War [1848–49 C.E.].The Sikh Empire dissolved after defeat in 1849 C.E.

Aphrodite: Aphrodite is the Greek goddess of love, beauty, pleasure, and procreation.

Arnavaz and Sharnaz: Arnavāz is one of the two daughters or possibly sisters of Jamšhid, the mythological king of Iran. Arnavāz and her sister, Sharnaz were kidnapped by Zahhak, who killed Jamšhid, but they later married Fereydun, after he had defeated Zahhāk.

Arnimaal: Arnimal [circa 18th century C.E.] was a leading Kashmiri Brahmin poet.

Arthur: King Arthur is a legendary British king who, according to medieval histories and romances, led the defence of Britain against Saxon invaders in the late 5th and early 6th centuries C.E.

Aru: It is a two-hour hike from Pahalgam, Srinagar and is known for its scenic meadows, lakes, and mountains besides being a base camp for trekking to the Kolahoi Glacier and the twin Tarsar and Marsar Lakes.

Arzhang Div: Arzhang Div is a character in Shahnameh. He is demon chief of Mazandaran in Rostam's Seven Labors and eventually Rostam killed him and rescued Kay Kāvus.

Atlas: In Greek mythology, Atlas was a Titan condemned to hold up the sky for eternity after the Titanomachy.

Avatar: Reincarnation of a god or goddess in any form as per Hindu mythology.

Awrad: Awrad-i-Fathia is one of these priceless compositions of Amir i- Kabir describing in a grand and sublime style, the grand attributes of the one and only God, Allah SWT and blessings on the Holy Prophet SAW. It is recited twice daily after Fajr [early dawn] and Isha [before going to bed] prayers at the Khaneqahi Maullah and after Fajr prayers in most of the mosques of the Kashmir valley.

Azaan: The *adhan* or Aadhaan is the Islamic call to worship, recited by the *muezzin* at prescribed times of the day. The main purpose behind the multiple loud pronouncements of Azaan in every mosque is to make available to everyone an easily intelligible summary of Islamic belief. The Azaan recites the *Takbir* [Allah SWT is great] followed by the *Shahada* [There is no God but Allah SWT and the Prophet Muhammad SAW is the messenger of Allah SWT]. This statement of faith, called the *Kalimah*, is the first of the Five Pillars of Islam.

Azadi: An Urdu word meaning Independence.

Bach: Johann Sebastian Bach [1685 – 1750 C.E.] was a German composer and musician of the Baroque period. He is now generally regarded as one of the greatest composers of all time.

Bakirkhwanis: Kashmiri bread similar to a round naan in appearance, layered with a smattering of sesame seeds. It is usually preferred with Noon Chai or Kehwa.

Bakshi: Bakshi Ghulam Mohammad [1907–1972 C.E.] was a politician belonging to the National Conference and served as the Deputy Prime Minister of the State of Jammu and Kashmir [1947–1953 C.E.]. He fell out with Sheikh Abdullah in 1953 and engineered a coup, after which he served as the longest serving Prime Minister of the State for eleven years, [1953 – 1964 C.E.].

Barmayeh: The special cow whose milk was used by Faranak to feed Fereydun.

Basilisk: A mythical lizard that has the power to kill human beings by a mere stare.

Beethoven: Ludwig van Beethoven [1770–1827 C.E.] was a German composer and pianist. A crucial figure in the transition between the Classical and Romantic eras in Western art music, he remains one of the most famous and influential of all composers.

Begar: Begar a form of unfree labour is a generic or collective term for those work relations, especially in modern or early modern history, in which people are employed against their will by the threat of destitution, detention, violence [including death], compulsion, or other extreme hardship to themselves or to members of their families and was started by Sikhs in Kashmir.

Bizhan and Manizeh: Bizhan is one of the main Iranian heroes in the Shahnameh. Bizhan is son of Giv and Banu Goshasp and grandson of Goudarz and Rostam. He is mostly famous for his role in the story of Bizhan and Manizeh, where he fell in love with Manizeh, the daughter of Afrasiab, the king of Turan and long-time enemy of Iran.

Black Dog: An evil-spirit dog that stalks the streets at night.

Boulevard: The landmark boulevard snaking around the shores of the Dal Lake in Srinagar.

Bulbul Shah: Hazrat *Bulbul Shah* [RA] the first Muslim saint to come to Kashmir from Turkistan. He was effective in converting Rinchana to Islam.

Bund: The Bund is a beautiful river facing market in Srinagar.

Cain and Abel: Cain [Qabil] and Abel [Habil] are believed by Muslims to have been the first two sons of Hazrat Adam[PBUH] [Adam] and Hazrat Hawah[PBUH] [Eve] mentioned in the Holy Qur'an. Cain killed Abel out of jealousy and lust.

CAT: An acronym for caught and trained militants in Kashmir made to work as armed forces collaborators and facilitators in anti-militancy operations.

Centaurs: Half-men and half-horse creatures which run wild and are unruly, considered staple creatures in European folklore.

Chanakya: Chanakya was an Indian teacher, philosopher, economist, jurist, and royal advisor. He is traditionally identified as Kauṭilya or Vishnugupta, who authored the ancient Indian political treatise, the *Arthashastra.*

Changthangi: The Changthangi or Pashmina goat [*Capra aegagrus hircus*] is a breed of goat inhabiting the plateaus in Tibet and neighboring areas of Ladakh in Kashmir. They are raised for ultra-fine cashmere wool known as pashmina once woven.

Char Chinari: Char Chinar, also rendered as Char Chinari, Ropa Lank, or Rupa Lank [Kashmiri – Silver Island] is an island in Dal Lake. The island located on the Bod Dal [Big Dal] is marked with the presence of majestic Chinar trees at the four corners, thus known as Char-Chinari [Four Chinars]. Murad Baksh, brother of the Mughal emperor Aurangzeb, constructed the Rupa Lank.

Che: Ernesto "Che" Guevara [1928–1967 C.E.] was an Argentinian Marxist revolutionary, physician, author, guerrilla leader, diplomat, and military theorist. A major figure of the Cuban Revolution, his stylized visage has become a ubiquitous counter-cultural symbol of rebellion and global insignia in popular culture.

Chole bhatoorey: Chole bhatoorey is a combination of chana masala and fried bread called bhatoora made from maida flour.

Charar-i-Sharif: Charar-i-Sharif is considered one of the most sacrosanct Muslim shrines in Kashmir. The Shrine of Charar-i-Sharif is approximately 600 years old and is the resting place of Hazrat Sheikh Noor-ud-Din Wali[A.S]

Chinar: *[Platanus orientalis]*, or oriental plane, is the state tree of Kashmir. The name is derived from Persian "Che Nar " – What Fire? Islamic preachers who travelled to Kashmir four centuries ago from Central Asia and Persia also revered the tree. It is said that the oldest Chinar tree in Kashmir, around 700 years old, was planted by the Sufi Saint Syed Qasim Shah in Chattergam, in central Kashmir's Budgam district.

Chiru: The Tibetan antelope or Chiru [*Pantholops hodgsonii*] is a medium-sized bovid native to the Tibetan plateau. They are hunted for their soft and warm wool which is known as *shahtoosh* and is used to weave Shahtoosh shawls in Kashmir. Shahtoosh is the world's finest wool having the lowest micron count, followed by Vicuna and Pashmina.

Conspiracy Case: Kashmir Conspiracy Case was the legal case filed by Government of Kashmir and Investigations Department of the Government of India, by which Sheikh Abdullah and others were arrested and jailed. Abdullah along with Mirza Afzal Beg and 22 others were accused of conspiracy against the state for allegedly espousing the cause of an independent Kashmir.

Crackdown: A term used by Kashmiris to describe the cordon and search operations conducted by Indian armed forces in Kashmir.

Curfew: A regulation requiring people to remain indoors between specified hours, typically at night but usually covering day-time too in Kashmir.

Cyclops: A one-eyed monster that captures and eats people alive.

Daksum: Situated at a height of 8500 feet, it is a trekker's paradise swathed in coniferous forests, gurgling streams, lush alpine meadows. It is also famous for its trout – an angler's heaven.

Dal: Dal is a world renowned lake in Srinagar [Dal Lake is a misnomer as Dal in Kashmiri means lake].The urban lake, which is the second largest in the state, is integral to tourism and recreation in Kashmir and is named the "Jewel in the crown of Kashmir" or "Srinagar's Jewel".

Damavand: The Mountain is said to hold magical powers in the *Shahnameh*. Damāvand has also been named in the Iranian legend of Arash as recounted by Bal'ami as the location from which the hero shot his magical arrow to mark the border of Iran, during the border dispute between Iran and Turan.

Danderwaan: A Kashmiri vegetable vendors shop.

Dara Shukoh : Dara Shukoh [1615 –1659 C.E.] was the eldest son and the heir-apparent of the fifth Mughal Emperor Shah Jahan but was defeated and later killed by his younger brother, Prince Muhi-ud-din [later, the Great Emperor Aurangzeb], in a bitter struggle for the imperial throne.

Dastgeer Sahib: Dastgeer Sahib is a two-century old shrine situated in khaniyar, Srinagar. Sheikh Syed Abdul Qadir Jeelani never stayed there. It has the old Quran written by Hazrat Abu Bakr Sidiq[R.A] and Hazrat Ali[A.S] and the *Moi –e-Pak* a hair strand of Sheikh Syed Abdul Qadir Jeelani.

Diaspora: Pandits settled across the globe especially those in India.

Dilli: Ancient name for Delhi which is officially the National Capital Territory of Delhi or NCT. It has been continuously inhabited since the 6th century BC and has served as a capital city for empires across centuries.

Div-e-Sepid: In the Persian epic of Shahnameh Div-e Sepid, or Div-e-Sefid literally "White Demon" is the chieftain of the Divs [demons] of Mazandaran. He possesses great physical strength and is skilled in sorcery and necromancy and destroys the army of Kay Kāvus by conjuring a dark storm of hail, boulders, and tree trunks using his magical skills. He then captures Kay Kāvus, his commanders, and paladins; blinds them, and imprisons them in a dungeon. The greatest Persian mythical hero Rostam undertakes his "Seven Labors" to free his sovereign. At the end, Rostam slays Div-e Sepid and uses his heart and blood to cure the blindness of the king and the captured Persian heroes. Rostam also takes the Div's head as a helmet and is often pictured wearing it.

Dogras: The Dogras are an Indo-Aryan ethno-linguistic group in India and Pakistan. Dogras ruled Jammu from the 19th century, when Gulab Singh was made a hereditary Raja of Jammu by the Sikh Emperor Maharaja Ranjit Singh. Through the Treaty of Amritsar [1846 C.E.], they acquired Kashmir as well. The Brahmin Dogras are predominantly Saraswat Brahmins, genetically of common origin with Saraswat Brahmins of Kashmir.

Doonga: A tribe of Kashmiris known locally as Haenz or boat people live in small houseboats called Doongas.

Dupatta: Dupatta is a long, multi-purpose scarf that is essential to many Kashmiri women's suits and matches the woman's garments.

Durrani's: The Durrani dynasty was founded in 1747 by Ahmad Shah Durrani at Kandahar and included present day Afghanistan, most of present-day Pakistan and Kashmir, as well as Punjab. In 1753, Abdul Khan Isk Aquasi, a general in Ahmed Shah Abdali's army, invaded Kashmir and established the rule of the Durrani Empire of Afghanistan. Afghan rule in Kashmir was extremely cruel and oppressive. Dominance of Afghans declined after Ahmed Shah Abdali's death in 1772, but they ruled Kashmir for another 47 years.

Dussa: A long, plain Kashmiri shawl worn exclusively by Kashmiri male's especially older ones who wrap it over their pherans or jackets. Two varieties are commonly used, the pashmina dussa or the rafal dussa, the former being the costlier one.

Eid: Eid can be either Eid-al-Fitr or Eid-al-Adha. Eid-al-Fitr "the festival of breaking of the fast" is an important religious festival celebrated by Muslims worldwide that marks the end of Ramadan, the Islamic holy month of fasting [*sawm*] and / or Eid-al-Adha "the festival of the Sacrifice', also called the "Sacrifice Feast", is the second of two Muslim festivals celebrated worldwide each year. It honors the willingness of Hazrat Ibrahim A.S to sacrifice his son, Hazrat Ishmael A.S as an act of submission to Allah SWT's command.

Elves: A race of humanoids that excels in sorcery as well as archery and distinguished by their pointed ears.

Emperor Akbar: Abu'l-Fath Jalal-ud-din Muhammad [1542 -1605 C.E.] popularly known as Akbar [literally "the great"] and later Akbar the Great, was the third Mughal Emperor from 1556 until his death and one of the greatest emperors that the world has seen.

Encounter: "Encounter "is a term used in Kashmir to describe extra judicial killings by the police or the armed forces, allegedly in self-defence, when they encounter suspected militants.

Erina: A much frequented Ice – cream parlor situated on the Residency Road, Srinagar.

Esfandiyar: Esfandiyār is a legendary Iranian hero. He was the son and the crown prince of the Kayanian King Goshtasp [Middle Persian: *Wishtasp* and Avestan: *Vishtaspa]* and brother of the immortal Pashotan [Middle Persian: Peshotan and Avestan: Peshotanu] Esfandiyār is best known from the tragic story of a battle with Rostam described in Ferdowsi's epic Shahnameh. It is one of the longest episodes in Shahnameh, and is one of its literary highlights.

Faranak: Fereydun's mother, Farānak is a female character in the Persian epic *Shahnameh*. She is the wife of Abtin and the mother of Fereydun. Farânak is derived from the word Parvâneh, which means butterfly in Persian.

Fawkes: Guy Fawkes also known as Guido Fawkes, was a member of a group of provincial English Catholics who planned the failed "Gunpowder Plot" of 1605 C.E. who planned to assassinate King James I and restore a Catholic monarch to the throne.

Fereydun: According to Ferdowsi's Shahnameh, Fereydun was the son of Ābtin, one of the descendants of Jamšhid. Fereydun, together with Kāve, revolted against the tyrannical king, Zahhak, defeated and bound him in a pit in the Alborz Mountains. Afterwards, Fereydun became the king, married Arnavāz and Sharnaz.

Ferigees: Siyavesh falls in love with and marries Ferigees ["Curly Locks"] or Farangis, Afrasiab's daughter, thereby sealing his new attachment to life at the Turanian Court.

Gandhi: Mohandas Karamchand Gandhi [1869 –1948 C.E.] was the pre-eminent leader of the Indian independence movement in British-ruled India. Employing nonviolent civil disobedience, Gandhi led India to independence and inspired movements for civil rights and freedom across the world. He is revered as the Father of the Indian Nation.

Gangabal: The Gangabal Lake is situated at the foothills of Mount Haramukh in Ganderbal district of Srinagar. It is an alpine high altitude oligotrophic lake with a length of two and a half kilometers and maximum width of one kilometer besides being home to many species of fish, including the brown trout.

Gnome: A breed of diminutive humanoids who dwell in the recesses below the earth's surface.

Goblin: A mythical creature, grotesque and abominable in appearance with an excessive greed for gold and jewels.

Gondola: Not the ones plying in Venetian canals but named after and an equally breathtaking cable car ride from Gulmarg to Khilanmarg and beyond.

Goorewaan: A Kashmiri dairy product seller's shop.

Grihastha: Grihastha literally means "being in and occupied with home, family", or "householder". It refers to the second phase of an individual's life in four age-based stages of the Hindu ashram system.

Grim Reaper: In European folklore, a Grim Reaper is considered to be a veritable representation of death, an entity that snatches away peoples souls and transports them to their after-life.

Gulab Singh: Gulab Singh [1792–1857 C.E.] was the founder of Dogra dynasty and the first Maharaja of the princely state of Kashmir, the second largest princely state in British India.

Gujjars: Gujjars are a pastoral agricultural ethnic group with populations in India and Pakistan and a small number in northeastern Afghanistan. They are present in considerable numbers in Kashmir.

Gulmarg: Gulmarg is a town, a hill station, a popular skiing destination in Kashmir and is situated in the Pir Panjal range in the western Himalayas. It was named *Gulmarg* ["meadow of flowers"] by Sultan Yusuf Shah of Kashmir who frequented the place with his queen, Habba Khatoon in the 16th century.

Habba Khatoon: Habba Khatoon [1554–1609 C.E.] was a sixteenth-century Kashmiri Muslim poet and ascetic, who is also known as 'Nightingale of Kashmir'. She was born in the small village of Chandhara near "Pampore" and was known by the name *Zoon* [the Moon] because of her mesmerizing beauty until her marriage with Yusuf Shah Chak, who later became the ruler of Kashmir, after which she was called Habba Khatoon. When her husband was captured by deceit by the Mughal emperor Akbar and sent away to Bengal she became an ascetic. She has a profound presence in the oral tradition and is hailed as the last independent poet queen of Kashmir.

Haft-Khan-e-Rostam: The Seven Labors of Rostam or Haft-Khan-e-Rostam is a series of acts carried out by the greatest of the Iranian heroes, Rostam. The story of Haft-khan was retold by Ferdowsi in his epic poem, Shahnameh. In his labors, Rostam was often accompanied only by his horse, Rakhsh.

Haj: The Haj is an annual Islamic pilgrimage to Makkah, the holiest city of the Muslims, and a mandatory religious duty for Muslims that must be carried out at least once in their lifetime by all adult Muslims who are physically and financially capable of undertaking the journey, and can support their family during their absence. It is one of the five pillars of Islam, alongside the Shahada, Salat, Zakat, and Sawm. The Haj is the largest annual gathering of people in the world.

Haj-i- Baitullah and Milad - ud - Nabi[SAW], Navroz, Muharram and Ramadan, Urs, Shab -i -Baraat and Shab-i- Qadr, Eid-ul- Fitr and Eid -ul -Adha: Kashmiri Muslim events and festivals.

Hara: Mount Hara is the place of refuge for Fereydun when he is sought for by the spies of Zahhāk.

Hari Parbat: Hari Parbat, or Koh-e-Maran, is a hill overlooking Srinagar and is the site of the Durrani Fort and has a notable religious dimension for the Hindus, Muslim and Sikhs alike, hosting two shrines of locally venerated Muslim saints, a famous Hindu temple and a Sikh Gurudwara.

Hartal: It is mass protest often involving a total shutdown of workplaces, offices, shops even courts of law as a form of civil disobedience usually at the instance of the militant and resistance organizations in Kashmir.

Harissa: A delectable minced mutton delicacy peppered with a varied assortment of spices and condiments and usually consumed in winters in Kashmir.

Hazratbal: The Hazratbal Shrine, literally meaning a "Majestic Place", is a Muslim shrine in Hazratbal, Srinagar. It contains a relic, the *Moi-e-Muqqadas*, believed by many Muslims of Kashmir to be a hair of Prophet Hazrat Muhammad SAW. The shrine is situated on the left bank of the Dal Lake, Srinagar and is considered to be Kashmir's holiest Muslim shrine.

Herath: Shivaratri, called 'Herath' in Kashmiri, a word derived from the Sanskrit 'Hararatri' the 'Night of Hara' celebrated with great fervour by Kashmiri Pandits.

Highlands: An iconic hotel in Gulmarg.

Houseboats: The houseboats in Kashmir were first constructed by Englishmen residing and visiting Kashmir as non-residents were not allowed to build and own houses. They are usually moored at the edges of the Dal Lake and Nagin lakes. These houseboats are delectable pieces of art and are made of wood and usually have intricately carved wood paneling. They are furnished with exotic walnut wood furniture, Kashmiri silk carpets and European chandeliers.

Hum Kya Chahtey: An Urdu slogan meaning "What do we want?" commonly used in anti-India protests.

Huma: The Huma is a mythical bird of Iranian legends and fables and continuing as a common motif in Sufi and Diwan poetry. Although there are many legends of the creature, common to all is that the bird is said to never alight on the ground, and instead to live its entire life flying invisibly high above the earth.

Hushang: In Shāhnāmeh, Hushang was the son of Siyāmak and grandson of Keyumars. He led the army against the son of Ahriman that avenged the death of Siyāmak. During Hushang's reign, many new discoveries were made for the comfort of humanity like iron and the principles of iron-working; the methods of agriculture and irrigation; he learned how to domesticate certain beasts as livestock and for use as draught animals; how to make clothing from the furs of other beasts; and he discovered how to make fire from flint.

IED: Improvised Explosive device.

Ikhwan: The organization of the Renegade militants in Kashmir.

Ilm-i-Din: It is the name given to knowledge and / or study of Islam.

In all things be men: The motto of the Valley's first and finest English medium school, the CMS Tyndale Biscoe School, established in 1880 by Rev. Knowles and is dubbed as the assembly line of Kashmiri talent.

Indus: The Indus River, also called Sindhū, is a major south-flowing river in South Asia. The total length of the river is 3,180 kilometers [1,980 miles] which makes it one of the longest rivers in Asia. Originating in the western part of Tibet in the vicinity of Mount Kailash and Lake Manasarovar, the river runs a course through Ladakh and Gilgit-Baltistan in Kashmir.

Iqamah: The word Iqamah or ikamet refers to the second call to Islamic Prayer, given immediately before the prayer begins. Generally, the iqamah is given more quickly and in a more monotonous fashion, compared to the adhan, as it is addressed to those already in the mosque rather than a reminder for those outside it to go to the mosque.

Islam: Islam is a monotheistic religion which professes that there is only one and incomparable God, Allah SWT and that Prophet Muhammad SAW is the messenger of Allah SWT. It is the world's largest religion [CIA World Book – as per practicing adherents] as well as the fastest-growing major religion in the world. Islam teaches that Allah SWT is merciful, all-powerful, and unique and He has guided mankind through revealed scriptures, natural signs, and a line of prophets sealed by Prophet Hazrat Muhammad SAW. The primary scriptures of Islam are the *Holy Quran,* viewed by Muslims as the verbatim word of God, and the teachings and normative example called the *Sunnah,* composed of accounts called *hadith* of Prophet Hazrat Muhammad SAW [570–632 CE].

Jago, Jago, Subeh Huwi: An Urdu slogan meaning "Wake up, wake up, the day has dawned" usually blared from mosque loudspeakers in Kashmir at the onset of the anti-India insurgency.

Jamia: Jamia Masjid is a mosque in Shehr-e-Khaas, Srinagar, Kashmir and was built by Sultan Sikandar Shah Shahmiri in 1394 AD.

Jamšhid: According to the Shahnameh, he was the fourth king of the world. He had command over all the angels and demons of the world, and was both king and high priest of Hormozd [middle Persian for Ahura Mazda]. From this time the *farr* departed from Jamšhid and he repented in his heart, but his glory never returned to him. Zahhak fought against, trapped and brutally murdered him.

Janus: In ancient Roman religion and myth, Janus is the god of beginnings, gates, transitions, time, duality, doorways, passages, and endings. He is usually depicted as having two faces.

Jannah: Jannah is the Islamic concept of paradise. The common interpretation is that it is an eternal place for the believers of tawhid.

Jee Enns: An iconic patisserie and bakery in Poloview, Srinagar.

JIC: Joint Interrogation centre, Interrogation centers set up jointly by Indian armed forces in Kashmir.

Judas: Judas Iscariot was, according to the New Testament, one of the twelve original disciples of Jesus Christ, known for the kiss and betrayal of Jesus to the Sanhedrin for thirty silver coins. His name is often used synonymously with betrayal or treason.

Kabootar Khana: Kabootar Khana is a small heritage palace constructed on a small island inside Dal Lake which used to be a famous holidaying spot.

Kadag xwaday: Commoners in ancient Persia.

Kahwa: Kahwa or Kehwa is a traditional Kashmiri beverage made by boiling kahwa tea leaves with saffron strands, cinnamon bark, cardamom pods and occasionally gulkand [a sweet preserve of rose petals, sugar and aromatic spices like cardamom and cinnamon] to add a great aroma. Generally, it is served with sugar or honey and crushed nuts, usually almonds and is prepared in a copper vessel known as a samovar and often served in tiny, shallow cups. Kahwa in Kashmir is also commonly served after Wazwan and elaborate family dinners.

Kalhana: Kalhana [Circa 12th century] a Kashmiri, was the author of *Rajatarangini* [*River of Kings*], an account of the history of Kashmir. He wrote the work in Sanskrit between 1148 and 1149 C.E.

Kanderwaan: A Kashmiri bakery.

Kanishka: Kanishka I [Sanskrit: Kaniṣka] or Kanishka the Great, was the emperor of the Kushan dynasty in the second century [Circa. 127–150 C.E.] Kanishka's reputation in Buddhist tradition regarded with utmost importance as he administered the 4th Buddhist Council in Kashmir. It was presided by Vasumitra and Ashwaghosha.

Karakuli: A Karakuli or qaraqul hat is made from the fur of the Qaraqul breed of sheep, often from the fur of aborted lamb fetuses. The triangular hat is part of the costume of the native people of Kashmir especially those belonging to the upper classes.

Kasheer: In the Kashmiri language, Kashmir is known as *Kasheer*. The ex-princely state of Kashmir denotes a larger area that nowadays includes the Indian administered territory of Jammu and Kashmir, the Pakistani administered territories of Azad Kashmir and Gilgit-Baltistan, and Chinese-administered territories of Aksai Chin as well as the Trans-Karakoram Tract. The Sanskrit word for Kashmir was *káśmīra*. The Ancient Greeks called the region *Kasperia* which has been identified with *Kaspapyros* of Hecataeus and *Kaspatyros* of Herodotus. Kashmir is also believed to be the country meant by Ptolemy's *Kaspeiria*. *Cashmere* is an archaic spelling of present day Kashmir.

Kasher: A Kashmiri female .This word is also used as a prefix for any Kashmiri female entity.

Kasher Koor: A Kashmiri [Kasher] girl [Koor].

Kashur: A Kashmiri male .This word is also used as a prefix for any Kashmiri male entity.

Kashyapa: Kashyapa is a revered Vedic sage of Hindu Mythology. He was one of the seven ancient sages [rishis] considered as Saptarishis in *Rigveda*, numerous Sanskrit texts and Indian mythologies. He is the most ancient rishi listed in the colophon verse in the *Brihadaranyaka Upanishad*, and called a self-made scholar in the *Atharvaveda*.

Kaula: Kaula, also known as Kula, Kulamārga ["the Kula practice"] and Kaulācāra ["the Kaula conduct"], is a religious tradition in Shaktism and tantric Shaivism.

Kaunsarnag: Kaunsarnag is a picturesque lake located at a height of 13,500 feet in South Kashmir and measures two and a half kilometers by about a kilometer in size.

Kay Kāvus: Kay Kāvus is a mythological Shah of Iran and a character in the Shāhnāmeh. He is the son of Kay Qobād and the father of prince Siyāvesh. Kāvus rules Iran for one hundred and fifty years during which he is frequently though increasingly grudgingly aided by the famous hero Rostam.

Keffiyah: Keffiyah is a traditional Middle Eastern headdress fashioned from a square scarf, usually made of cotton. It is typically worn by Arabs, as well as by some Mizrahi Jews and Kurds. In recent times Kashmiri protestors have taken to wearing them in substantial numbers.

Khaneqah: A Khanqah or Khaneqah is a building designed specifically for gatherings of a Sufi brotherhood or *tariqa* and is a place for spiritual retreat and character reformation. In the past, and to a lesser extent nowadays, they often served as hospices for saliks [Sufi travelers], Murids [initiates] and talibs [Islamic students]. Khaneqahs are very often found adjoined to dargahs [shrines of Sufi saints], mosques, and madrasas [Islamic schools].

Khayam: A movie theater in downtown Srinagar.

Khedive: The term Khedive is a title largely equivalent to the English word viceroy, governor, or in some cases an overlord.

Khilanmarg: Khilanmarg is a small valley about a 6-km walk from the Gulmarg .The meadow, carpeted with flowers in the spring, is the site for Gulmarg's winter ski runs and offers a fine view of the surrounding peaks of the great Himalayas from Nanga Parbat to the twin 7,100-metre peaks of Nun and Kun to the southeast.

Khosrow and Shirin: Khosrow and Shirin is the title of a famous Persian tragic romance by the Persian poet Nizami Ganjavi [1141–1209 C.E.] and tells a highly elaborated fictional version of the story of the love of the Sassanian king Khosrow II for the Armenian princess Shirin, who becomes queen of Persia. The essential narrative is a love story of Persian origin which was already well-known from the Shahnameh.

Khune Asyavushan: Siyāvesh, a noble Iranian prince is suspected of treason by Afrasiab, who orders his execution by beheading. Peeran, the Grand Vizier, emplores the Emperor, not to commit the horrendous mistake of killing the innocent. "Do not make thyself a flag upon this

Earth." Afrasiab ignores this warning and the execution is carried out swiftly. As Siyavesh's blood reaches the ground, a plant grows upon the same spot and is later named "Khune Asyavushan," or the "blood of Siyavesh."

Khvarenah: Khvarenah is an Avestan word for a Zoroastrian concept literally denoting "glory" or "splendour" but understood as a divine mystical force or power projected upon and aiding the appointed ruler.

Koh-i-Maran: Another name for Hari Parbat Mountain in Srinagar.

Kokernag: The name of Kokernag originates from Koh [Mountain] kan [from or under] nag [spring]. Kokernag is at the height of approx. 2,000 meters above sea level and is known for its beautiful gardens, largest fresh water springs in Kashmir and for its largest rainbow trout hatchery in the subcontinent.

Koshur: Kashmiri or Koshur is a language from the Dardic subgroup of the Indo-Aryan languages and it is spoken primarily in the Kashmir Valley and Chenab valley of Kashmir.

Lal Ded: Lalleshwari, Lalli-Arifa, [1320–1392 C.E.] was a mystic of the Kashmiri Shaivite sect. She was a creator of the mystic poetry called vatsun or *Vakhs*, literally "speech" [Voice]. Each unit is a stanza of three lines followed by a refrain [vooj] Known as Lal Vakhs; her verses are the earliest compositions in the Kashmiri language and are an important part in history of modern Kashmiri literature. She inspired and interacted with many Sufis of Kashmir.

Lal Sheikh: An all-inclusive restaurant on the Bund, Srinagar.

Lalitaditya: Lalitaditya Muktapīḍa [reigned 724 CE–760 C.E.] was the most powerful ruler of the Karkoṭa Empire of Kashmir region in the Indian Subcontinent. The dynasty exercised influence in northwestern India from 625 C.E. until 1003 C.E.

Leprechaun: A mythical creature generally represented as a diminutive man with a long beard that hides a treasure on the other end of rainbows.

Lernaean Hydra: The Lernaean Hydra or Hydra of Lerna was a serpentine water monster in Greek and Roman mythology. In the canonical Hydra myth, the monster is killed by Heracles, more often known as Hercules, using sword and fire, as the second of his Twelve Labors.

Lidder: Lidder is a 73 kilometers long river in South Kashmir. It originates from the Kolahoi glacier and joins the Jhelum River.

LMG: Light Machine Gun

Lol: Habba Khatun introduced "lol" to Kashmiri poetry; "lol" is more or less equivalent to the English 'lyric'. It conveys one brief thought.

Machiavelli: Niccolò Machiavelli [1469 –1527 C.E.], or more formally Niccolò di Bernardo dei Machiavelli, was a Florentine Renaissance historian, politician, diplomat, philosopher, humanist, and writer. He has often been called the founder of modern political science. He wrote his most renowned work *The Prince* [*Il Principe*] in 1513 C.E.

Madinah: Madinah was Prophet Hazrat Muhammad SAW's destination after his SAW's Hijrah from Makkah and became the capital of a rapidly increasing Muslim Empire, first under Prophet Hazrat Muhammad SAW's leadership, and then under the first four Rashidun caliphs. It served as the power base of Islam in its first century where the early Muslim community developed.

Madrassa: Madrassa is the Arabic word for any type of educational institution, whether secular or religious. However, it is usually used for schools dealing with religious studies.

Magadha: Magadha is a region in the Indian state of Bihar and formed one of the sixteen Mahajanapadas [Sanskrit: "Great Countries] of ancient India.

Mahadev: Mahadev or Mahadev peak is a mountain peak in the vicinity of the Dachigam National Park in Srinagar and is the highest peak at 13013 feet [3966 meters] of the Zabarwan range.

Makhdoom Sahib: Hamza Makhdoom Kashmiri, popularly known as Makhdoom Sahib [Circa 1494–1576 C.E.], was a Sufi mystic, scholar, and spiritual teacher living in Kashmir. He is sometimes referred to as Mehboob-ul-Alam and Sultan-ul-Arifeen.

Makkah: As the birthplace of Prophet Hazrat Muhammad SAW and the site of his SAW first revelation of the Holy Quran, Makkah is regarded as the holiest city of Islam and a pilgrimage to it known as the Hajj is obligatory for all able Muslims. Makkah is home to the Kaaba, by majority description Islam's holiest site, as well as being the direction of Muslim prayer.

Manasbal: Manasbal Lake is located in Ganderbal District in Kashmir. The lake is stated to be the deepest lake at 13 meters or 43 feet in the sub-continent. The large growth of lotus [*Nelumbo nucifera*] at the periphery of the lake adds to the beauty of the resplendent waters of the lake. The Mughal garden, called the Jaroka built by Empress Nur Jahan overlooks the lake. The lake is a good place for bird watching as it is one of the largest natural stamping grounds of Aquatic birds in Kashmir and has earned the sobriquet of "supreme gem of all Kashmir Lakes".

Masala lavasa rolls: A Kashmiri snack prepared by rolling boiled red beans in the traditional tandoor bread called lavasa.

Matador: Local mini-buses plying in Srinagar.

Mate Roze: One of the most melodious songs sung by Shameem Dev, an accomplished female singer from Kashmir renowned for her exceptionally melodious voice.

Mattan: It is the location for the famous Martand Sun Temple in Kashmir.

Maulvi: Maulvi or Mawlawi is an honorific Islamic religious title given to Muslim religious scholars or Ulema preceding their names, similar to the titles Maulana, Mullah, or Sheikh.

Mazandaran: In Shahnameh, Mazandaran in the land of great Divs [demons]. It is such a horrible place that no Shah of Iran dared to go there and conquer the land.

Mazda: Local mini buses plying in Srinagar.

Medusa: In Greek mythology Medusa was a monster, a Gorgon, generally described as a winged human female with living venomous snakes in place of hair. Gazers upon her hideous face would turn to stone.

Mehfil: A highly rated restaurant at Poloview, Srinagar.

Mehrab: Mehrab or Mihrab is a semicircular niche in the wall of a mosque that indicates the *qibla*; that is, the direction of the Kaabah in Makkah and hence the direction that Muslims should face when praying. The wall in which a *mehrab* appears is thus the "*qibla* wall".

Mihirakula: Mihirakula was one of the most important Hephthalite emperors, whose empire was in the present-day territories of Afghanistan, Pakistan, and northern and central India. After being defeated by the king Yasodharman of Malwa in 528 and the Gupta emperor, Narasimhagupta Baladitya, who previously paid him tribute. Mihirakula was taken as prisoner, and later released, but meanwhile the brother of Mihirakula had seized power over the Hephthalites. Mihirakula set off for Kashmir where the king received him with honor. After a few years Mihirakula incited a revolt against the king of Kashmir and seized his power. Mihirakula is remembered amongst Buddhist writers "as a terrible persecutor of their religion".

Minotaur: In Greek mythology, the Minotaur was a creature with the head of a bull and the body of a man or, as described by Roman poet, Ovid, a being "part man and part bull". The Minotaur dwelt at the center of the Labyrinth, which was an elaborate maze-like construction designed by the architect Daedalus and his son Icarus, on the command of King Minos of Crete. The Minotaur was eventually killed by the Athenian hero, Theseus.

Mlecchas: Mleccha [Vedic Sanskrit word meaning "non-Vedic", "barbarian"] is a name, which referred to people of foreign extraction in ancient India. The term is used to describe all "undesirable outsiders".

Moi-e-Muqaddas: The relic, the *Moi-e-Muqqadas*, stored in the Hazratbal shrine in Srinagar, is believed by many Muslims of Kashmir to be a hair strand of the Prophet Hazrat Muhammad SAW.

Monje Gaade: A Kashmiri snack prepared by deep frying small sized fish covered with rice and gram flour batter and mild spices.

Mountbatten: Admiral of the Fleet, Louis Francis Albert Victor Nicholas Mountbatten, 1st Earl Mountbatten of Burma, [born Prince Louis of Battenberg; 1900 –1979 C.E.] was a British naval officer and statesman. During the Second World War, he was Supreme Allied Commander, South East Asia Command [1943–46 C.E.]. He was the last Viceroy of India [1947] and the first Governor-General of independent India [1947–48 C.E.]

Muezzins: A muezzin is the person appointed at a mosque to lead and recite the call to prayer.

Mughals: The Mughal Empire or Mogul Empire was the largest ever empire in the Indian subcontinent, established and ruled by a Muslim Turkic dynasty of Chagatai Turko-Mongol origin from Central Asia. They won over the local populace, kings, and emperors either by battle or by offering generous terms of subordination, religious tolerance, and meritocracy. Their age is qualified as a classical age in India.

Mughal Darbar: A much hyped bakery in Poloview, Srinagar.

Mukhbir: A government or an armed forces mole within the civilian populace or militant organizations in Kashmir.

Nadr-e-Monje: A Kashmiri snack prepared by deep frying lotus stems coated with a mixture of gram and rice flour and smattered with mild spices.

Namdas: A **Namda** is a thick, warm woolen rug, mostly embroidered and is widely acclaimed to have originated during 11th century when Akbar, the great Mughal ruler was on throne. The art of felting wool into namdas has been sourced from Yarkand.

Naush Daru: The healing potion that KayKavus delayed giving Rostam to revive a fatally wounded Sohrab.

Navreh and Herath, Pan and Gaade Batte, Gengah Atham, Tila Atham and Huri Atham, Khetsimavas, Zyeath Atham and Zarma Satham, Tiky Tsoram, Vyetha Truvah and Anta Tsodah: Kashmiri Pandit festivals celebrated with fervour and frolic by Kashmiri pandits.

Nikah: In Islam, marriage is a legal contract between two people. Both the groom and the bride are to consent to the marriage out of their own volition. A formal, binding contract is considered integral to a religiously valid Islamic marriage, and outlines the rights and responsibilities of the groom and bride. There must be two Muslim witnesses of the marriage contract.

Nishat: Nishat Bagh is a terraced Mughal garden built on the eastern side of the Dal Lake, close to Srinagar. It is the second largest Mughal garden in the Kashmir Valley. 'Nishat Bagh' is Urdu, which means "Garden of Joy," "Garden of Gladness" and "Garden of Delight.

Nonnus: Nonnus of Panopolis was a Greek epic poet of Hellenized Egypt of the Imperial Roman era.

Noon Chai: It is a traditional salt tea from Kashmir. It is a part of Kashmiri culture to drink this beverage on a daily basis with traditional Kashmiri breads and pastries like lavasa, sheermal, kander tchot, bakirkhwani or kulcha.

Nund Reshi: Nund Rishi or Nund Reshi is also known as Sheikh Noor ud-Din Wali and popularly as Sheikh Ul-Alam among the Muslim and as Sahajanand and among the Hindus. He was a Kashmiri mystic regarded as the patron saint of Kashmiris. He is considered to be founder of the Rishi order of saints which deeply influenced many great mystics like Hamza Makhdoom, Resh Mir Sàeb and Shamas Faqir till present day.

Ogre: An ugly, oversized and overbearing creature blessed with great physical prowess coupled with diminutive intelligence.

Op Tupac: Code name given to an operation planned by General Zia-Ul-Haq of Pakistan to execute armed insurgency in Kashmir and named after the legendary Túpac Amaru or Thupa Amaro [1545–1572 C.E.] who was the last indigenous monarch [Sapa Inca] of the Neo-Inca State, remnants of the Inca Empire in Vilcabamba, Peru and led the anti-Spanish resistance.

Pahalgam: It is a popular tourist destination and the most beautiful Kashmiri hill station located on the banks of Lidder River at an altitude of 7,200 feet [2,200 meters].There are various trekking and hiking spots accessible from here alongwith a host of mighty peaks.

Paladin: Holy Persian warrior like Rostam.

Pampore: Pampore is a historic town situated on the eastern side of river Jhelum on Srinagar-Jammu National Highway in Kashmir. It is famous across the globe for its Saffron [Crocus sativus] the world's costliest spice by weight.

Pandit: Jawaharlal Nehru [1889–1964 C.E.] was the first Prime Minister of India and a central figure in Indian politics before and after independence. He is considered to be the architect of the modern Indian nation-state: a sovereign, socialist, secular, and democratic republic. He was also known as Pandit Nehru because he and his ancestors belonged to the Kashmiri Pandit community.

Pandits: The Kashmiri Pandits are a Shaivite Saraswat Brahmin community from the Kashmir Valley.

PAPA 2: Papa 2 was an interrogation centre in Kashmir operated by the Border Security Force, one of the Indian armed forces, from the start of the Kashmiri insurgency in 1989 until it was shut down in 1996 due to the exhaustive list of human rights abuses perpetrated out there.

Pari Mahal: The Pari Mahal was built by Mughal Prince Dara Shikoh on the Zabarwan Mountain above Chashma Shahi in Srinagar in the mid-1600s. It served as a library and an abode for him. It was further used as an observatory, useful for teaching astrology and astronomy.

Pashmina: Pashmina is a fine type of cashmere wool. The woolen shawls made in Kashmir are mentioned in Afghan texts between the 3rd century BC and the 11th century AD. The textiles made from it were first woven in Kashmir. The name comes from Persian *pašmina*, meaning "made from wool" and literally translates to "Soft Gold" in Kashmiri. Pashmina came to be known as "Cashmere" in the West because Europeans first encountered this fiber in Kashmir.

Patel: Sardar Vallabhbhai Patel [1875 –1950 C.E.] was the first Deputy Prime Minister of India. He was an Indian barrister and statesman, a leader of the Indian National Congress and a founding father of the Republic of India who played a leading role in the country's struggle for independence and guided the integration of princely states into a united nation though in many cases by questionable means.

Pather Masjid: Pather Masjid, known locally as *Naev Masheed* [Kashmiri: New Mosque] is a Mughal era stone mosque located in the old city of Srinagar. It was built by Mughal Empress Nur Jehan, the wife of Emperor Jahangir.

Pheran and Poatsch: The traditional outfit for both males and females in Kashmir is the Pheran and Poatsch. The Pheran and Poatsch are two gowns, worn one over the other. The traditional Pheran and Poatsch extend to the feet, which was popular up to the late 19th century. However, a relatively modern variation of the Pheran and Poatsch extends below the knees, which is worn with a shalwar.

In summer, the Pheran and Poatsch are made of cotton, but in winter, the Poatsch is made out of cotton and the Pheran of wool, covering and protecting the body from the cold.

Pir-a-Vaer: The garden of saints. A sobriquet bestowed upon Kashmir.

Pishachas: Pishachas are flesh-eating demons in Hindu mythology. They have been described to have a dark complexion with bulging veins and protruding red eyes. They are believed to have their own languages, known as Paiśāci. According to one legend, they are sons of Kashyapa and Krodhavasa, one of the daughters of Prajapati Daksha.

Pishdad: Pishdadian is the first dynasty of Iranian people in the *Shahnameh,* Avesta and Iranian mythology. The Pishdadian Dynasty is said to have produced the first kings who ruled over the land of Persia. Some of the Pishdadian kings are thought to have ruled for thousands of years and include Keyumars, Hushang, Jamšhid, Fereydun and Manuchehr etc.

Poloview: One of the poshest shopping areas in Srinagar, the capital of Kashmir.

Prang: Prang village is meant for its natural and enthralling beauty. The main attraction of this village is its garden, which attracts the tourists throughout the year. This village is also famous for its clear streams, cold air, and mighty mountains

PSA: The Public Safety Act, is one of the most draconian laws applicable in Jammu and Kashmir, that is being liberally used as a tool of repression to scuttle any dissent and often also for victimizing innocent youth.

Puffs: A variety of crisp, layered Kashmiri bread.

Pujwaan: A Kashmiri butcher shop.

Qasim: Syed Mir Qasim was the Chief Minister of Kashmir [1971–1975 C.E.]

Quisling: A quisling is a person who collaborates with an enemy occupying force or more generally as a synonym for traitor and originates from the surname of the Norwegian war-time leader Vidkun Quisling, who headed a domestic Nazi collaborationist regime during the Second World War.

Quran: The Holy Quran literally meaning "the recitation"; is the central religious text of Islam, revealed by Allah SWT through his Archangel Hazrat Jibreel[A.S] [Gabriel] to the Prophet Hazrat Muhammad SAW over the course of 23 years. The Quran is divided into 30 chapters or Paras.

Qurbani: *Qurbānī* as referred to in Islamic law is the sacrifice of a livestock animal during Eid al-Adha or for other specific occasions.

Radh: Floating gardens, labelled the 'Radh' in the Kashmiri language are a special feature of the Dal Lake. They basically constitute of matted vegetation and earth, but are floating. These are detached from the bottom of the lake and drawn to a suitable place and anchored. Given its rich nutrient properties, tomatoes, cucumbers, and melons etc. are grown.

Raghu Ram Kaul: He was an ancestor of Sheikh Muhammad Abdullah, an ex-Prime and Chief Minister of J&K state, who converted to Islam in 1722 C.E., as per Abdullah's autobiography *Atish-e-Chinar.*

Rajatarangini: *Rajatarangini* [Sanskrit Rājataraṃgiṇī, "The River of Kings"] is a metrical legendary and historical chronicle of the north-western Indian subcontinent, particularly the kings of Kashmir. It was written in Sanskrit by Kashmiri historian Kalhana in the 12th century C.E. The work consists of 7826 verses, which are divided into eight books called *Tarangas* ["waves"].

Rakhsh: Rakhsh meaning luminous is the stallion of protagonist Rostam in the *Shahnameh* and was considered to be the strongest and the most faithful horse in the world.

Rediwallahs: Kashmiri street food vendors.

Renegades: Kashmiri militants turned government collaborators largely due to the lure of the lucre. They are considered to be an abomination in Kashmir largely because of an allegedly huge corpus of atrocities and killings of innocent civilians by them.

Residency: One of the high-end shopping areas in Srinagar and takes its name from the British-era Resident's quarters.

Rhubab: Rhubab is a lute-like musical instrument originating from central Afghanistan and played by Kashmiri Gujjars and musicians.

Rinchana : Rinchan, whose full name was Lhachan Gualbu Rinchana, was a Buddhist prince from Ladakh, and the son of the Ladakh chief, Lhachan Ngos-gruba, who ruled Ladakh [1290–1320 C.E.] He revolted against his uncle, the ruler of Ladakh, but was defeated and fled to Kashmir. Raja Suhadeva appointed Rinchan as a minister. Mongols under their leader Dulchaa invaded Kashmir and defeated Suhadeva, who fled to Tibet after which his prime minister, Ramachandra, took advantage of the anarchy and occupied the throne. He appointed Rinchan as an administrator. Rinchan became ambitious and sent a force in the fort in the guise of merchants, who took

Ramachandra's men by surprise and killed him and his family were taken prisoners. Rinchan became the ruler of Kashmir. Rinchan converted to Islam and adopted the title of Sultan Sadruddin Shah. Ten thousand of his subjects, including his brother-in-law Ravanachandra, converted along with him.

Roodabeh: Roodabeh is a Persian mythological female figure in Shahnameh. She is the princess of Kabul who later marries Zal. They had two children, including Rostam, the main hero of the Shahnameh.

Rostam: Rostam is the most celebrated legendary hero in Shahnameh and Iranian mythology. In Shahnameh, Rostam is best known for his tragic fight with Esfandiyar, the other legendary Iranian hero, for his expedition to Mazandaran including his labors and for his mournful fight with his son, Sohrab, who was killed in the battle. He was the son of Zal and Roodabeh.

Rouf: It is a form of traditional Kashmiri dance performed usually by women on occasions like marriages and festivals like Eid and Urs of various saints etc.

RPG: Rocket propelled grenade.

Sadiq: Ghulam Mohammed Sadiq [1912–1971 C.E.] was the Prime Minister of Jammu and Kashmir [1964–1965 C.E.], when the position was renamed to Chief Minister which he continued till 1971.

Sahrdaran, vaspuhran, wuzurgan and azadan: The aristocracy and nobility in Persia of yore.

Salah-o-Quran: It refers to Islamic prayers and recitation of the Holy Quran.

Sangbaaz: Another name for Kashmiri youth who pelt stones at Indian armed forces as a form of protest against the violation of human rights.

SantRam: A well-known eatery in Amira Kadal area in Srinagar.

Saraswat Brahmins: The Saraswats are a sub-group of Hindu Brahmins who trace their ancestry to the banks of the mythical Saraswati River.

Satyr: A mythical creature usually represented as being a half-man and a half-goat and notorious for being wild and lustful.

Seekh tuji: A popular Kashmiri mutton based barbeque.

Sewaiyan kulfi: A Kashmiri ice-cream variant made up of sev, milk, ice and sugar.

Shabdiz: Shabdiz meaning "night-colored" or "black" was the legendary black stallion of Khosrow Parvez, one of the most famed Sassanid Persian kings [reigned 590–628 C.E.] and was considered to be the fastest horse in the world.

Shab-i-Baraat: It is a night of prayers observed by Muslims and falls on the night between 14th and 15th of Sha'ban, as per the Hijri Calendar. It is regarded as a night of forgiveness and also when the fortunes of the Ummah for the coming year are decided.

Shab-i-Qadr: Laylat-al-Qadr variously dubbed as the Night of Decree, Night of Power, Night of Value, Night of Destiny, or Night of Measures, is in Islamic belief the night when the first verses of the Quran were revealed to the Prophet Hazrat Muhammad SAW. It is observed on the odd nights of the last ten days of Ramadan. Muslims believe that on this night the blessings and mercy of Allah SWT are abundant, sins are forgiven, supplications are accepted, and that the annual decree is revealed to the angels who also descend to earth.

Shabrang: In Persian mythology, Shabrang, literally meant "night-coloured purebred", was the horse of the hero Siyāvesh and was considered to be the noblest horse in the world.

Shahada: The *Shahada,* "the testimony"; *aš-šahādatān or* the two testimonials" also *Kalima Shahadat* is an Islamic creed declaring belief in the oneness of Allah SWT [*tawhid*] and the acceptance of Prophet Hazrat Muhammad SAW as the messenger of Allah SWT.

Shahnameh: The *Shahnameh,* also transliterated as *Shahnama* ["The Book of Kings"], is a long epic poem written by the Persian poet Ferdowsi between Circa 977 and 1010 C.E. and is the national epic of Greater Iran. Consisting of some 50,000 "distichs" or couplets, the *Shahnameh* is the world's longest epic poem written by a single poet. It tells mainly the mythical and to some extent the historical past of the Persian Empire from the creation of the world until the Islamic conquest of Persia in the 7th century.

Shahtoosh: Shahtoosh [also written shahtush, a Persian word meaning "king of fine wools"] is the name given to a specific kind of shawl, which is woven with the wool of the Tibetan antelope [Chiru], by master craftsmen and women of Kashmir. The Shahtoosh shawl is now a banned item with possession and sale being illegal in most countries for the Chiru is an endangered species under CITES. The estimated market value of one Shahtoosh shawl in the western market is around $6000–9000. Shahtoosh is the world's finest wool having the lowest micron count, followed by Vicuna and Pashmina.

Shaivism: Shaivism is one of the major traditions within Hinduism that reveres Shiva as the Supreme Being or its metaphysical concept of Brahman. The followers of Shaivism are called "Shaivas" or "Saivas". It considers both the Vedas and the Agama texts as important sources of theology.

Shakti: A famous confectionary and sweets shop in Regal Chowk, Srinagar.

Shalimar: Shalimar Bagh is a Mughal garden in Srinagar, linked through a channel to the northeast of Dal Lake, on its right bank located on the outskirts of Srinagar. Its other names are Farah Baksh and Faiz Baksh. The Bagh was built by Mughal Emperor Jahangir for his wife Nur Jahan, in 1619 C.E. The Bagh is considered the high point of Mughal horticulture.

Shamsuddin: Shams-ud-Din Shah Mir [reigned 1339–42 C.E.] was a ruler of Kashmir; and the founder of the Shah Miri dynasty, which is named after him. Shah Mir is believed to have come to Kashmir during the rule of Suhadeva [1301–1320 C.E.], where he rose to prominence. After the death of Suhadeva and his brother Udayanadeva, Shah Mir established his own kingship, founding the Shah Mir dynasty in 1339 C.E., which lasted till 1561 C.E.

Shameem Dev: Shameem Dev Azad is a famous female singer from Kashmir acclaimed globally for her melodious voice and is the wife of Ghulam Nabi Azad, former Chief Minister of Jammu and Kashmir.

Shamiyana: A popular restaurant at the entrance to the Boulevard in Srinagar.

Shankaracharya: The Shankaracharya Temple also known as the Jyesteshwara temple or Pas-Pahar by Buddhists and is situated on the top of the Takht-e-Suleiman or Shankaracharya Hill on the Zabarwan range in Srinagar.

Shape shifters: Humans who can willingly take the form of animals while maintaining their consciousness.

Sheen-e-jung: Kashmiri word for snow fight.

Sheikh: Sheikh Mohammed Abdullah [1905 –1982 C.E.] was a Kashmiri politician who played a central role in the politics of Kashmir. Abdullah was the founding leader of the National Conference and agitated against the rule of the Maharaja Hari Singh and urged self-rule for Kashmir. He was the Prime Minister of the state of Jammu and Kashmir after its accession to India in 1947 and was later jailed and exiled. He was dismissed from the position of Prime Ministership on 8 August 1953 and again became the Chief Minister of the state following the infamous 1974 Indira-Sheikh accord.

Sheermal: Kashmiri version of flat bread used in marriage parties and celebratory events. The best ones come from Pampore on the outskirts of Srinagar.

Shehr-e-Khaas: The "downtown" or the old city of Srinagar, also known as Shehr-e-Khaas. It has the greatest assortment of arts and crafts factories and retail dealerships. It showcases traditional Kashmiri architecture and town planning and is a cultural repository too.

Sher Garhi: Sher Garhi Palace or the Tiger Fortress is a palace in Srinagar. Sher Garhi means 'tiger fortress' and was constructed as a fortress and a palace by the Afghan governor, Jawansher Khan in 1772 C.E.

Shikara: The shikara is a type of wooden boat found on Dal Lake and other water bodies of Srinagar. Shikaras are of varied sizes and are used for multiple purposes.

Shikarawallahs: Men and sometimes women plying the shikaras in the Dal Lake in Srinagar.

Shrukhe: Sheikh Nur-ud-din used his poetry as tool to spread the knowledge of the "Absolute". His poetry is commonly known as *Shrukhe. Tawhid, Risala, Ma'ad,* human lust are main subjects of his poetry. His sayings are preserved in the NurNama, written by Baba Nasib-ud-din Ghazi in Persian about two centuries after his death. One of his most famous and oft-quoted couplets is [Kashmiri: "Ann poshi teli yeli wann poshi"] meaning 'Food shall last as long as the forests last ".

Sikander: Sikandar Shah Miri better known as Sikandar But-Shikan ["Sikandar the Iconoclast"] was the sixth sultan of the Shah Miri dynasty of Kashmir. He ruled the kingdom from 1389 to 1413 C.E.

Simurgh: The Simurgh made its most famous appearance in the Ferdowsi's epic *Shahnameh* where its involvement with the Prince Zal is described. Zal was the albino son of Sam who abandoned him at *Alborz* where he was reared by a Simurgh, a bird of gigantic proportions. When he rejoined the world, she gave him three golden feathers which he was to burn if he ever needed her assistance.

Siyāmak: Siyāmak was a son of Keyumars who died at the hands of Ahriman's son.

Siyavesh: Siyâvoš in Persian and Avestan Syâvaršan is a major figure in the *Shahnameh*. He was a legendary Iranian prince from the earliest days of the Iranian Empire. A handsome and desirable young man, his name literally means "the one with the black horse" or "black stallion". Siyavesh is the symbol of innocence in Iranian literature. His defence of his own chastity, self-imposed exile, constancy in love for his wife, and ultimate execution at the hands of his adopted host, Afrasiab, have become intertwined with Iranian mythology and literature over the past millennia. In Iranian mythology, his name is also linked with the growth of plants.

Soanthe: The Kashmiri name for spring.

SOG: The Special Operations Group [SOG] is a 1000-strong elite anti-insurgency force chosen from more than 100,000 troopers of the Jammu and Kashmir Police. It was raised in 1994 and since then the J&K police has been on the frontlines in anti-militancy activities.

Sohrab: Sohrāb is a character from the Shahnameh in the tragedy of Rostam and Sohrab. He was the son of Rostam, who was an Iranian warrior, and Tahmineh, the daughter of the king of Samangan. He was slain at a young age by his father Rostam who only found out he was his son after fatally wounding him in a duel.

Somanand: Somananda [875–925 C.E.] was one of the teachers of Kashmir Shaivism, in the lineage of *Trayambaka,* author of the first philosophical treatise of this school, *Sivadrsti.* A contemporary of *Bhatta Kallata,* the two formed the first wave of Kashmiri Shaivites to propose in a rigorous and logical way the concepts of non-dual Shaivism.

Sonamarg: Sonamarg [literally "Meadow of Gold"] is an alpine valley situated at the bank of Nallah Sindh is a popular tourist destination in Kashmir and prides itself on playing host to the great Himalayan glaciers of Kashmir Valley namely Kolahoi Glacier and Machoi Glacier with some peaks of above 5000 meters, like Sirbal Peak, Kolahoi Peak, and Machoi Peak.

Srinagar: Srinagar is the largest city and the summer capital of the Indian administered state of Jammu and Kashmir. It lies in the Kashmir Valley on the banks of the Jhelum River. The city is famous for its gardens, waterfronts, and houseboats and is also known for traditional Kashmiri handicrafts, fruits, and dried fruits. The Burzahom archaeological site located 10 km from Srinagar has revealed the presence of Neolithic and Megalithic cultures making it one of the oldest and continuously inhabited cities in the world.

Standstill: A standstill agreement was an agreement signed between the newly independent dominions of India and Pakistan and the princely states of the British Indian Empire prior to their integration in the new dominions. The princely state of Kashmir, which was contiguous to both India and Pakistan, decided to remain independent. It offered to sign standstill agreements with both of the dominions.

Sudabeh: Sudabeh is a character in the Persian epic *Shahnameh.* She is a princess of Hamavaran kingdom [Saka Haumavarga or Amyrgian] and later, becomes the wife of Kay Kāvus, Shah of Iran, and stepmother of prince Siyavesh. She is most famous for her role in Siyavesh choosing exile after he spurns her sexual advances. She blamed Siyavesh for rape with the help of her witches. Siyavesh proved innocent goes to Turan where he is assassinated and later Rostam, who blames Sudabeh for the incident, kills her.

Suhadeva: Suhadeva [reigned 1301–1320 C.E.] was a weak Kashmiri Hindu King. During his reign, a Tatar chief, Dulchaa invaded Kashmir and ravaged it. King Suhadeva fled the country and his general Ramachandra occupied the throne.

Sunset Peak: Sunset Peak also known as Romesh Thong is a mountain massif with a peak elevation of 4,745 meters [15,568 feet] in Shopian, Kashmir. It is the highest peak of this massif and as the name suggests lies in the west of the Vale of Kashmir as a whole.

TADA: Terrorist and Disruptive Activities [Prevention] Act. It was the first anti-terrorism law legislated by the government to define and counter terrorist activities. The Act was widely criticized by human rights organizations as it contained provisions violating human rights.

Tahmineh: Tahmineh is a female character in the Shahnameh. Her name is mentioned as the wife of Rostam and as the daughter of Samanganshah, the sovereign of Samangan. She is the mother of Sohrab.

Takht-e-Sulaiman: Another name for the Shankaracharya hill in Srinagar.

Tamerlane: Timur [1336—1405 C.E.] historically known as Amir Timur and Tamerlane was a Turko-Mongol conqueror and founder of the Timurid Empire in Persia and Central Asia. Timur considered to be the last of the great nomadic conquerors of the Eurasian Steppe, referred to himself as the "Sword of Islam". By the end of his reign, Timur had gained complete control over all the remnants of the Chagatai Khanate, the Ilkhanate, and the Golden Horde, and even attempted to restore the Yuan dynasty in China.

Tandoor: The term tandoor refers to a variety of ovens but here it refers to the ones used by bakers in Kashmir.

Tanzeem: Generic Kashmiri/Urdu name for a militant organization in Kashmir.

Tao's: A quaint restaurant alongside the Bund, Srinagar.

Tarsar and Marsar: The Tarsar Lake or Tar Sar is an almond-shaped, oligotrophic alpine lake situated in the Kashmir Valley, specifically in Aru and is dominated by the peaks of the Kolahoi Mountain. The lake is separated by a mountain with a minimum peak elevation of 4,000 meters [13,000 feet] from another lake of the same nature known as Marsar Lake, which is in the vicinity of Dachigam National Park.

TDC: Refers to Tourist development Corporation of J&K State.

Tehreek: Anti-India insurgency led by local Kashmiri youth.

Titan: In Greek mythology, the Titans and Titanesses were members of the second generation of divine beings, descending from the primordial deities and preceding the Olympian deities.

Trika: Trika, a concept of Kashmir Shaivism, refers to the three goddesses Parā, Parāparā and Aparā which are named in the *Mālinivijayottata-tantra.* This gives Kashmir Shaivism its other name, Trika.

Treaty of Amritsar: The infamous Treaty of Amritsar, signed on 16 March 1846, formalized the arrangements in the Treaty of Lahore between the British East India Company and Gulab Singh Dogra after the First Anglo-Sikh War. By Article I of the treaty, Gulab Singh acquired "all the hilly or mountainous country with its dependencies situated to the eastward of the River Indus and the westward of the River Ravi including Chamba and excluding Lahaul, being part of the territories ceded to the British Government by the Lahore State according to the provisions of Article IV of the Treaty of Lahore, dated 9th March, 1846." Under Article III, Gulab Singh was to pay 75 lakhs [7.5 million] Nanak Shahi rupees [the ruling currency of the Sikh Empire] to the British Government, along with other annual tributes. The Treaty of Amritsar marked the beginning of Dogra rule in Kashmir.

Tower of Babel: The Tower of Babel is recorded in the Jewish Tanakh's first book [Genesis] and is meant to explain the origin of different languages.

Troll: An ugly cave-dwelling creature depicted as either a giant or a dwarf.

Tulmul: Kheer Bhawani is a temple dedicated to the goddess Kheer Bhawani near the village of Tulmul in Kashmir.

Turan: Tūrān literally means "the land of the Tur", and is a region in Central Asia. The term is of Iranian origin and may refer to a certain pre-historic human settlement, a historic geographical region, or a culture. The original Turanians were an Iranian tribe of the Avestan age.

Umayyads: The Umayyad Caliphate [Arabic – *Al-Khilāfah al-'umawiyya*], was the second of the four major caliphates established after the death of Prophet Hazrat Muhammad SAW. At its greatest extent, the Umayyad Caliphate covered 11,100,000 km^2 [4,300,000 square miles] and 62 million people [29% of the world's population], making it one of the largest empires in history in both area and proportion of the world's population.

Umrah: The Umrah is a pilgrimage to Makkah performed by Muslims that can be undertaken at any time of the year, in contrast to the Hajj that is performed only in the month of Dhul-Hajja. In the *Sharia*, Umrah means to perform *Tawaf* round the Kaaba and *Sa'i* between Al-Safa and Al-Marwah, after assuming *Ihram* [a sacred state], from a *Miqat*. The Umrah is not compulsory but highly recommended.

Valkyries: Mythical Scandinavian female deities with the power to choose warriors to die in battle and transport their souls to Valhalla.

Vampire: A mythical creature in human form that hunts other humans to suck their blood.

Venus: Venus is the Roman goddess whose functions encompassed love, beauty, desire, sex, fertility, prosperity, and victory. In Roman mythology, she was the mother of the Roman people.

Verinag: A major tourist attraction of this place is Verinag Spring, for which this place is named. The spring is the major source of river Jhelum. There is an octagonal stone basin at Verinag Spring and an arcade surrounding it which was built by Mughal emperor Jahangir in 1620 C.E. Later, a beautiful garden next to this spring, was laid out by his son Shah Jahan. This spring is known to never dry up or overflow.

Vicuna: The vicuña [*Vicugna vicugna*] or vicugna is one of two wild South American camelids which live in the high alpine areas of the Andes and produce small amounts of extremely fine wool, which is very expensive because the animal can only be shorn every three years. When knitted together, the product of the vicuña's wool is very soft and warm.

Vitruvian Man: The *Vitruvian Man* or simply *L'Uomo Vitruviano* is a drawing by Leonardo da Vinci around 1490 C.E. depicts a man in two superimposed positions with his arms and legs apart and inscribed in a circle and square.

Wande: A Kashmiri word for winter.

Wanvun: It literally means "chorus" and is basically a style of singing used to sing Kashmiri folk songs. Wanvun is an integral part of marriage and any welcoming ceremonies.

Wendigo: An extremely evil being that overtakes the human entities and transforms them into cannibals.

Werewolf: It is a mythological or folkloric human with the ability to shape shift into a wolf or a hybrid wolf-like creature, either purposely or after being placed under a curse or affliction.

Wular: Wular Lake is one of the largest fresh water lakes in Asia. In ancient times, Wular Lake was also called Mahapadmasar and is referred as *Bolor* by Al-Biruni [960–1031 C.E.]. The lake, with its big dimensions and the extent of water, gives rise to high leaping waves in the afternoons, called Ullola in Sanskrit, meaning "stormy leaping, high rising waves". The origin may also be attributed to a Kashmiri word 'Wul', which means a gap or a fissure, an appellation that must have come also during this period.

Yogi Shahpore: The keeper and chief priest of the large temple built in the heart of the city of Srinagar by Raja Parversen in the second century C.E. The learned Hindu Sadhu wielded great influence on the Hindu masses and also on the Hindu intelligentsia. The great Yogi accepted Islam amidst a large gathering. This in turn resulted in mass conversions of Pandits to Islam.

Youp: Kashmiri word for flood.

Yusmarg: Yusmarg or Yousmarg is a hill station in the western part of Kashmir Valley. Yusmarg in Kashmiri means *The Meadow of Jesus* A.S and it is believed by Kashmiris that Prophet Hazrat Isa A.S [Jesus] came to Kashmir and stayed at Yusmarg for some time. It is an alpine valley covered with snow clad mountains and the meadows of Pine and Fir.

Yusuf Shah: Yusuf Shah Chak was a ruler of Kashmir and ruled Kashmir from 1579 to 1586 C.E. He soundly defeated the great Mughal Emperor Akbar twice and that too with a much smaller army. He was confined by deceit by Akbar after promising negotiations and safe return.

Zabarwan: The Zabarwan [Kashmiri: literally the good forest] Range is a short [20 miles or 32 kilometers long] sub-mountain range between Pir Panjal and Great Himalayan Range in the central part of the Kashmir Valley.

Zahhak: Zahhāk or Bevar Asp [Persian: meaning "he who owns tens of thousands of horses"]is an evil figure in Iranian mythology, evident in ancient Iranian folklore as Aži Dahāka, the name by which he also appears in the texts of the Avesta. In Zoroastrianism, Zahhak [going under the name Aži Dahāka] is considered the son of Angra Mainyu, the foe of Ahura Mazda. He murdered Jamšhid, kidnapped Arnavaz and Sharnaz and was later defeated, bound and kept in a pit by Fereydun

Zain-ul-Abidin: Ghiyas-ud-Din Zain-ul-Abidin [reigned: 1418–1419 C.E. and 1420–1470 C.E.] was the eighth *sultan* of Kashmir. He acquired a halo in popular imagination which still surrounds his name in spite of the lapse of nearly five hundred years. He was known by his subjects, and indeed still is, as *Bad Shah* [the Great King]. The first thirty-five years of his reign are described by Jonaraja in the *Rajatarangini Dvitiya,* while the subsequent years are described by Jonaraja's pupil, Srivara, in the *Rajatarangini Tritiya.* He abolished *Jaziya,* much before Emperor Akbar, which was levied on the Hindu majority of Kashmir. He extended liberal patronage to the Sanskrit language and literature. *Mahabharata* and Kalhana's *Rajatarangini* were translated into Persian on his order. Sultan Zain-ul-Abidin gave a fillip to arts and crafts of Kashmir by inviting craftsmen from adjoining Samarkand and other Central Asian cities. Papier Machie, wood carving, embroidery, and metallurgy *et. al* got a huge boost.

Zal: Zāl is a legendary Iranian King who hailed from Baluchistan and is recognized as one of the greatest warriors of the Shahnameh epic. Zāl came from a family, whose members were legendary warriors, who for generations, served in the Persian army as great generals. His father, Sām and, later, his son, Rostam were great heroes of Persia.

Zereh, Joshan and Babr-e-Bayan: Babr-e Bayān or Palangine is the name of a suit that Rostam, the legendary Iranian hero wore in wars. It was invulnerable against fire, water, and weapon. Rostam, before going to battle, wore three levels of defensive suits, he first put on a zereh, then a *gabr* or *joshan*, and lastly the Babr-e Bayan.

Zero Inn: A quaint snack parlor near the old zero bridge in Srinagar.

Zino of Citium: Zeno of Citium [Circa 334 – Circa 262 B.C.] was a Hellenistic thinker from Citium, Cyprus, and probably of Phoenician descent. Zino was the founder of the Stoic school of philosophy, which he taught in Athens from about 300 B.C.

370: Article 370 of the Indian Constitution is an article that grants a special autonomous status to the state of Jammu and Kashmir.

Made in the USA
Columbia, SC
07 August 2017